T0159003

I Am Alpha and Omega!
The Beginning and The End,
The First and The Last!

My Visit to Heaven
Book 1

Timothy

authorHOUSE®

AuthorHouse™
1663 Liberty Drive
Bloomington, IN 47403
www.authorhouse.com
Phone: 1 (800) 839-8640

Published by AuthorHouse 09/07/2018

ISBN: 978-1-5462-5890-2 (sc)
ISBN: 978-1-5462-5889-6 (e)

Print information available on the last page.

This book is printed on acid-free paper.

Dedication

I Timothy, unworthy servant and repentive sinner of The Most High God.

Dedicate This Seven Book Series, starting with this, first book, to all the peoples of the world.

If there was a great flood, which in fact there was. And if Noah and his family were those on the arc chosen to repopulate the planet, which they were!

Then who are we to each other? and to whom do we belong? if not to The Holy Trinity! The One True God!

Are we not all the same? and do we not all have the same Father? Do we not all share the same blood lines?

The greatest gift is Christ! So that we may all share in Gods' eternal Love and be covered by heavenly glory, forgiveness and mercy!

We shall wear the robe of righteousness eternally as unworthy as we are because we belong to Christ Jesus our Lord and Savior. The Holy Trinity is pure and perfect love. Now and forever!

May God bless you all and all whom you love. Have Faith, be Strong and Believe!

Amen!

While praying to God my Father I must have fallen asleep. I was awakened by three angels. I saw the angels glowing in heavenly glory and I trembled on my knees. "Do not be afraid Timothy", the angels replied. They picked me up off my knees. "We have been sent to you by God". "Come with us!" one of the angels replied. "We will show you the things from the very beginning before time existed. The things that have been hidden from the ages" replied the other. "Some things you will write for man to question and seek and other things you shall keep secret for they are the mysteries that shall reveal themselves to man after the day of judgment". I agreed to what the angels were asking of me and the angels took me.

I was surrounded by my heavenly hosts and the angels looked up towards heaven. Then before I knew what was happening, we traveled up the great tunnel of light as if going thru a suction. As we traveled you can see the earth below you and then the universe which has an end. It is like a bed sheet and can be rolled up and put away. We went higher and we past the third plain and went thru the second plain of creation. We saw the spirits of those who had died as they waited for the permission to enter heaven. The demons were there as well in judgment and accusing man for every sin and as false witnesses against the spirits. However, be not afraid for the angels were there in control guiding everyone thru the hall of halls. We kept going higher and there were bright lights full of all the different colors in the spectrum and many more that have not been seen yet by man. The closer we got to entering heaven the more ecstasy all of the five senses were in. The fullness of all things was filled within me. I felt great power, fulfillment and full satisfaction in all things and behold we rose right thru what seemed to be heavens floor.

For the first time, I felt complete. I remember thinking I felt perfect. "Come with us", said the angels and I followed them hovering above the floor yet walking at the same time. There was no solid floor as we know it on earth. Yet the floor even though it was a white light and cloudy it was solid and there was no way to fall down or fall thru the floor. It was solid yet none existent to the eye. The angels brought me before two doors and they turned to me saying. "There is non-worthy to enter, however you have found favor with The Holy of Holy for the greatness of your love".

As the doors were opened by the angel's commands, there were guardian angels on each side of the opening. They were dressed in bright armor. There were beasts that looked like lions and powerful other beasts not seen before roaring thru the white walls as a warning to all who entered. I was scared and entered fearing the unknown. I was shaking yet I felt strong. I was afraid yet I felt calm. I was at peace and very excited at the same time. "Behold the thrones of The Holy Trinity" the angels replied in perfect harmony. I saw bright lights each of 77 times 7 suns before me, blinding me as I lost all power and fell to my knees. However, my soul sensed The Holy Trinity and was in fear and ecstasy at the same time. While on my knees weeping with joy, Gods' voice thundered and shook the walls of heaven as I was asked to come forth.

The angels helped me up and brought me before the throne of the all mighty and I fell to my knees again. It was like I was 5000 years old and I couldn't carry myself or stand up straight. I was completely powerless yet I was filled with all things. I felt fear as I approached the throne of The Lord yet I was at peace at the same time. But most of all, my heart was bursting with pure love. My love poured out of me as a stream. Yet at the same time streams of love were pouring into me from the thrones of God. I was blanketed and then I was light. It's like I was transformed I had a new body or form with new eyes that can see all things and behold. I heard The Holy Trinity clearly giving me permission to gaze my unworthy eyes upon God. I was able to now see Jesus the Christ at the right hand of God sitting on His throne. In the Middle I saw God the Father. He was sitting on His glorious throne and The Holy Spirit was there towards the left of God. The Holy Spirit has a separate form and sits to the left of God yet is around God the Father and God the Son all at the same time. God is an infinite form and all creation seemed like it was alive in God for you saw all the forms of creation alive in God and at the same time God had a shape as a perfect man figure, as Jesus the Christ. The Holy Trinity is perfect and the most beautiful vision that my unworthy eyes, ever looked upon.

The Lord looked different than God the Father slightly. He looked like fine polished brass with holes in his hands and feet dressed in heavenly glory with flames of fire coming out of His eyes yet I can see his kind, loving and forgiving eyes. At the same time, the eyes showed great power, strength and judgment. There were great scents and colorful lights coming up from what seemed to be the floor of heaven before the thrown of God and was being laid before The Holy Trinity. I asked God. What is that which smells so wonderful and the lights that seemed alive arising before the thrown of the all mighty? God replied, "These are the prayers of the faithful and their repentance. Truly repented hearts prayers and cries of mercy are offered before us like incense and are pleasing to us. We accept them and offer those worthy, the blessings, that are worthy to each. This is the path of life for all creation". God said, child of I, there will be many questions and you will have the answers in time for the day of judgement is coming upon the earth and all inhabitants thereof".

With a loud thundering voice God called forth The Archangel Michael. Michael came thru the door and came by my side. Michael was bigger than the other angels and looked very powerful. He has no shape yet he is in white form. As He turns towards you see a face and communicates with His brothers telepathically. This is true with all the angels. They can also take a more solid form and look just like you and me if needed but only with Gods permission. I'm sure The Holy Trinity can communicate in many ways with all of creation. For everything was created by the word of God who is Jesus Christ. All of creation has been given life by The Holy Spirit who is God.

I Am Alpha and Omega! The Beginning and The End,
The First and The Last!

There are no words that can describe in detail what I have seen however I will try my best to describe what I have seen. Just remember, man has very limited vocabulary, knowledge and experience to understand all things pertaining to God and Gods work. One thing that I truly now know is that we do not know anything what's so ever. Did you know that the angels have been created to serve and worship man? Not know but when we are a completion in heaven. Yet, under Gods command they are always working behind the scenes and serving us. We all will be like little Gods' complete and will become the real children of God in every way after the glorious day of judgement. Then Gods word will be complete. ("Let us make him in our image....").

God commanded Michael to take me to the hall of the past ...The angels serve us since the beginning of their creation. But under Gods commandment. Michael takes me from the hand and helps me raise to my feet. I didn't want to leave and fell to the feet of Christ kissing them. The Lord our God looked down on me smiling and placed His hand on my head blessing me and purifying my heart while God and The Holy Spirit agreed. God thundered His voice and said to Michael "behold Lucifer's' replacement for his love for Me is pure and real. Bring him to the hall of the past and let him witness all the secrets since the time I Am and the very beginning of all creation". Please understand that the language spoken in heaven is NOT any of the languages we know here on earth. It was a different language yet I understood it. When I spoke, I spoke that language verbally and telepathically. Yet my brain translated it in English, Greek and Hebrew. I don't even know Hebrew.

Michael picked me up and took me away from Gods thrown so fast and before I can blink I was in the hall of the past. "Sit on the throne of knowledge" said Michael. "Your journey of creation begins". I need a pad and a pencil to take notes I said eagerly. "No need said Michael" all things will be written in you and you will be able to recall all things only when God allows you to. The secrets of the kingdom are not for all and never throw the pearls before the swine. Yet if a secret does fall upon an unworthy ear, it shall not be remembered by that being and God will wipe it out of the mind". I understand I eagerly replied. Michael stepped back and when he did so, I was on the throne of knowledge yet I couldn't see the throne I was feeling. I was in pure white light. There was white everywhere and never ending.

Then I heard Gods thundering voice, "let our light withdraw within its self and let there be darkness beneath us". Then the light withdrew into itself forming a white plain and there was darkness underneath and became a second plain running in a straight line underneath the light. Then God commanded that dark plain to separate and double forming a third plain of dark light running underneath the second. Then God said let my kingdom be formed and be alive as it multiplies eternally. Let it expand unlimitedly for all eternity and let it have no end. Let all the lights shine there off always and let there be a gold basin before me in all splendor with the flame of life that can't be extinguished full of unquenchable life". Then this beautiful gold like basin with a living fire appeared within the kingdoms hall we were in. The basin and the fire were alive. God then commanded the flame to form the first of all creation and with a thundering voice I heard, Lucifer! Come forward! Then this figure came walking out of the flame. He was beautiful and so bright in light. "Let all creation be free with will and let none be a slave to the other but instead be one with each other" commanded God. Lucifer's figure formed As Lucifer stepped forward out of the basin he turned and noticed his being on the shiny basin and smiled in pride of his splendor. Then Lucifer went to God and stood right by his side. "Let the eternal flame God commanded birth forth all my angels and my heavenly beings that will occupy Our kingdom and serve Us in righteousness". The Us God was referring to was Himself, Jesus who is The Christ of God and His Holy Spirit. NOT Lucifer! With this command angels and heavenly beings were birthed from the fire some with many wings others with many eyes. There were others that looked like different animals like lions and eagles yet they were very different however similar. All of the occupants of heaven came forth from the eternal flame and kept occupying heaven. Then God commanded the kingdom to separate into halls and rooms that He will walk thru and personally name and create within the walls. The kingdom of heaven is a living being, it multiplied within itself as God commanded. Its pure splendor and perfection and is truly alive. You see, all that has been created is within God himself. Everything created that is within God was done so by His word who is Jesus The Christ who also came within God and has always been one with God for The Christ is The Living Word of God in the flesh. The kingdom of heaven is occupied with all living things with free will. Each creation will be judged on that glorious day of judgment. Everything created by God full of splendor and power and with free will. Everything. Even the universe that is alive has free will and must stand judgment and be purified to be eternal. If not, it will be rolled up and wiped out of existence. Can you imagine the universe just being dead and done? Being wiped out of existence? That's how easy it is for God. Just a word. We are sons of God. We also have the power to create with our words and our actions. We have been given the gift of creation. With our love and faith, we are united with the Holy Trinity and so, we speak things into creation with a word and then followed by our actions we form a present and future. All of creation whether angel or being, non-were in the splendor of the first that was birthed by the eternal flame. Think about this. God creates all things with words. We are so special to God that He actually formed us with word and touch and then breathed into us a soul. A soul is a part of God and will then be returned to Him that it belongs too. Give to Cesar that which is Cesar' and on to God that which is Gods. We are judged on the delivery if you will. God witnessed the eternal flame birthing the occupants of heaven as God commanded those beings to form shapes and appearances with powers and abilities. With just his word who in fact is Jesus the Christ. When all was done it took a period yet it was not a measurable time for time is and was nonexistent to The Eternal God. But if you were to place a human time period for the understanding of all. The number would be seven days. On the seventh day, the halls and rooms and the beings of the eternal never ending heaven were all one. God then walked thru the rooms and prepared them. I will not go thru the details of all the rooms because of the amount of time it will take explain them all however I will share with you the few most important for now. Obviously the most important room is the room of Gods throne. It is there The Holy Trinity sits and there where God judges and sees all things. It is there that the prayers of all the believers with true repentance come before God as incense before His feet and Throne. There you will find the seven spirits of God and the fullness of the Holy Trinity. That huge room that has no boundaries as far as my eyes can see in every direction, has beast like creatures and different types of angels around the throne and these beings occupy the space. Each waiting for a command from God. Whether telepathically or in a loud thunderous and soothing sound. The room is white surrounded by bright lights yet all is visible. The colors are much more then we know in our spectrum and are harmonious to the eyes and not blinding. Yet the lights are perfect to gaze upon and your soul rejoices in the perfected splendor. The scent in the eternal room is everything great you can imagine. All in one harmonious perfected scent. You can smell all the flowers, all the fruit, all the sweetest food and the scents of all creation all rolled up together as one occupying your senses of smell as the colors occupied your sense of sight in full ecstasy. It is pure perfection. You feel like you are walking/ hovering over soft clouds beneath your feet as it seems as if it's a white floor. There is no start or finish yet you can't fall or go thru it. It is solid yet at the same time it is not there as a floor we walk on here on earth. It doesn't feel hard yet soft and solid, smooth and perfect without a single troublesome feeling. There is no physical weight, no pressure on your back or knees either. It's like walking on water without it wetting your feet. No cold or hot. The temperature as we call it is perfect. There is no sweat or cold there is no clothes yet your covered by a robe that seems to be alive and one with you. There is food and you eat. There is no waste or use of a bathroom. For everything consumed in Gods kingdom is perfect and all is great. The wine is like nectar and you never get drunk. The fruit is the sweetest and juiciest yet you don't get dirty you need no shower and still it is consumed by you totally and there is nothing that comes out of you as waste. It is all perfect and is all good. It becomes one with you. There are things to eat on Gods table of all creation. The difference between eating it here and enjoying it in the kingdom of heaven in all its splendor, is that it is perfect in heaven without the imperfections of this world. Everything, in heaven is perfected and fulfill the fullness of all your senses at the same time. The room of water pours forth the liquid of life that looks like a gold water fall with no end and no beginning. That room is reserved with a gold cup that has a long handle in perfected light. You will see Saint John the Baptist there. He baptized we in heavenly water and gave me to drink from it with His Holy Hand. I tell you this, that he who drinks of that water will never be thirsty again. Yet your spirit drives you back for more because of how perfect and delicious it is. You can drink and eat as much as you want. You can never get full. We know each other in the kingdom of heaven. Yet we are not male or female with organs and parts or with sexual desires. We are all one family with purified brothers and sisters and The Holy Trinity our Father. There is no desire for anything bad just pure perfection and delight of your being and senses. You can speak using the tongues of the angels or any other language you chose to whomever. We all understand all things and know all things and communicate fully with each other. There are no imperfections with our bodies. No limping or lack of limbs. No wheelchairs or walkers. There are no illnesses, sicknesses or disease. Most of all there is no death but only eternal life. It doesn't matter we understand all things and we know all things. We are all connected as one yet we are individuals at the same time. All of creation breathes the breath of life in the rhythm of Gods breath and we have been perfected to be there by our Lord and Savior Jesus Christ. You choose to communicate telepathically if you will. You can walk and go to the distances away from Gods throne room but you have this sense of urgency to go back because your love misses Him. There are other rooms or areas of heaven that the floor looks as if it is gold or full of all rubies and diamonds and precious stones. There is the room of water where it seems as if its confined in this big sectional surrounded with windows that will open and the water will pour forward. There is the room of visional creation as I call it where it seems your walking not in but on top of the universe with stars beneath your feet. So, imagine being on top of the universe walking on the stars and the planets but watching the whole universe thru a crystal-clear floor. Even the room is darker so you may enjoy the splendor of God's creation as if you are in a dark movie theater and your screen is the clear floor that is on top of the universe. Just so you know the universe is a flat plain. It looks like a splendid map. It will be rolled up and made done with if God chooses. So even though it keeps birthing and expanding as God commanded there is an end as there is a beginning. There is no fear or emotions. The only thing you feel is love and a connection to God in soul body and spirit.

There is another room called the gathering. Think of this room as a huge never-ending meeting room where Gods warrior angels and guardian angels meet and execute Gods plans. In this room, when you walk in, it seems that there is just enough space for you. Then as others show up, it's enough space for all of you. Then more come and yet you are all in the room and you all fit comfortably. It's like a self-expanding room that tailors itself according to the guest list. I will tell you briefly about another very special room of Gods. Lucifer and no angels were ever or shall ever be allowed in until its fulfillment on the day of judgement. This is the room of souls. It is sealed by God and there are massive angels on watch outside of it constantly for non-to enter. God gave permission for me to enter. As I entered I saw a beautiful what seemed as fine gold and bras polished in perfection huge basin that was alive. It roared with lion heads and shrieked with eagle screams it had eyes all around it saying Holy, Holy, Holy is The Lord in all His Heavenly Glory. I smiled and replied amen. My heart is always bursting with Love for The Holy Trinity. I was allowed to approach and look within. As I looked within I saw God and when he breathed into the basin as He did with Adam, the basin would birth a soul. Imagine, Gods breath, births souls that come from heaven and take on the flesh of man so that the blood lines can be purified. These souls were not our souls for our souls are multiplied from the original which was Adams and the blood lines. These were the souls of the holy who would have great parts in Gods plans. I placed my hands on the basin with a thank you and in love and I left the room in peace. I can't speak to much further about this room and what I have seen. Then there is the room of the Holy Apostles. A king is each, sitting on great thrones in glorious light. They are a sun each, in heavenly splendor. Crowns of glory upon each head and robes of stars covering them each. They are there waiting for the day of judgement as they bear witness of the children of Israel and the twelve tribes. Moses shall judge them as the apostles shall judge the 12 tribes. They are Christ like in fine polished brass and fire coming from their eyes yet you can see their eyes and their smile. There are so many rooms but I shall leave more for the next time. Let us now focus on how man cleansed heaven before he was even created. With that in mind we will now get an understanding of Lucifer and how the angels were created. We will see the war in heaven and what led up to it. Again, there is so much yet it will require many books. However, what I have seen is really hard to put in words or describe because I am limited in so many ways in the flesh and in this world, as we all are. So, I will use words known to try to help you understand what it was like or what I have seen. The words or the ability to communicate in that level does not exist here on earth. I believe that was a big reason Solomon asked God for knowledge. Not only to rule Gods people with a little error as possible, remember he is still human so he is imperfect but also to understand more of Gods perfection. You'll see Solomon walking with David and communicating in our Fathers kingdom. Even though as men they were imperfect they do wear the crowns of glory now in perfection. Now let's begin with the birth of the angels and the death of the fallen. The war that took place in heaven was a spiritual one and not one of blood and death. It was a rebellious siege of jealously and pride. The good angels came against Lucifer and his followers. They were pushed away from God as a wall closing upon you and God commanded their exile. As God commanded heavens floor was opened and they were thrown out of heaven as they fell like lightning from heaven. If it was not one of blood and death. If that was the case satan and the others would have been killed and would not exist today. Their job is an important one. They serve God even now without their knowledge of doing so. There most important job is to sift man and to separate the good from the evil in the blood lines. The evil will stand judgement and die. God gave the angels gifts and certain powers. Even though the fallen betrayed God their powers were not taken from them. However, their actions have been made limited with boundaries. All will be judged on the last day which in fact will also then birth forth the first day of eternal life where all things will have been made new and perfect according to Gods plan and intention. The rebellion in heaven purified and freed heaven of those angels that did not want to be there as servants and those that want to be servants of God and man. The fallen angels, the demons, want man to worship and serve them. God has created the angels to serve not to be served. God made us in His image not the angels. Yet Lucifer and his comrades wanted to be served by man. In essence, it was as if they had or desired to be above God and have God serve them. There trying to do this by having man serve satan and in his twisted and wicked being, it is like having God serving him because we are in Gods image. In fact, this one time, it became so bad that God had to open the windows in the room of water and drown man and have him start all over again because of how bad satan controlled man and man blindly served the fallen ones. Let us start from the beginning. I will try my best to paint a clear picture in your minds. But here on earth I see know how very limited were in every way and how the devil rejoices in our unperfected humanity that can only be perfected thru Christ Jesus our Lord. I am telling you the truth. The Holy Trinity is The One True God. God calls forth His first of all creation. Lucifer! come forth from My eternal flame in My heavenly splendor! It seemed like gold liquid was formed into shape and a figure stepped forward from the flame in beauty and splendor. As lucifer walked towards God he took a glimpse at himself on the gold basin holding the eternal flame and smiled full of pride being the first in such beauty. You are the first of all created angels, you are the angel of light. No other shall compare to your splendor and glory and you shall be by my side. You will be in charge of those who come after you. Then God called forth the eternal flame to birth forward all heavenly occupants and protectors of the seals and thrones. Behold, the flame of the eternal. Start birthing forward one after another occupant of heaven God commanded the eternal flame which is alive. There was none as splendid as lucifer neither in beauty, light or stature for he was beautiful, huge and powerful. God made him so for he was supposed to be Gods executioner of His will. Kind of like His right hand or top general He was to be right behind God eternally and by His righthand. God loved him so and made him great with a free will. Then the guardians of the throne and the heavenly hosts were created. Creatures with many eyes to watch all things and others short in stature yet powerful hovering above the thrown and the eternal flame birthed forth heavenly hosts and all the angels. Each in stature according to Gods reason and duty for each. Lucifer in the angelic language commanded all to line up before the throne of God and to worship their creator and thank God for all things. They all had free will. It was one of the greatest gifts given them. They also have access and the right to move thru the three plains. The angel's new things and understood things. They were given access to the room of knowledge where creation was explained and understood all of creation and the use of all things. However even though all in the room of knowledge was the words of God alive on a scroll bright in gold and moving there was no mention of the third plain and man. There was however the understanding of a second plain or the spiritual realm. So, the angels were given right to come and go between the two plains. The lord went down first into the second plain and commanded the light to fill the plain and to separate itself into sections and rooms and as you moved further away from God the dimmer and lonelier the light got and your feeling and connection to God started to diminish. When Christ was done the ceiling of the second plain opened and The Lord raised Himself up threw the floor of the throne room. He sat on His throne on the right side of the throne of Our father God. On the left hand of God and surrounding or blanketing the Father and The Son is The Holy Spirit. If you're thinking that I have seen God and see him you are right. However, that is for another discussion at another time. Lucifer didn't line up before Gods throne with the rest but stood right behind God in an angle between The Lord Jesus and God so he can witness their worship as all kneeled before God except Lucifer. He felt so good watching all kneel and felt as if they were kneeling for him. He quickly glimpsed towards Gods throne and then back again. He had this look not of jealously but how a child would be in a candy store. Ready to consume all the sugar until he becomes sick. He wondered, how much God must love me over everyone else to have created me in this splendor. The other angels were mesmerized by Lucifer's beauty and light. Such splendor such power such perfection. They knew they would follow his order for he is Gods Top General. It was evident. There was one who wasn't impressed and not trusted Lucifer from the very beginning. His name is Michael. Michael is huge just like lucifer and very powerful. Gabriel, Uriel and a few others noticed lucifer's smirks as well. They bowed their heads and listened to God as God welcomed them to His eternal splendor. The angels above sang the hymns and songs of heaven as there was a celebration of the birth of all created and heaven celebrated in peace and in harmony. They all got a chance to know their creator and were filled with His love knowledge and care. When their spirits were filled with Gods love for them, one was not impressed. He felt that this is a weakness for one who rules. So lucifer didn't open himself and his free will completely to God and did not fill with the creator's eternal fullness. Anyway, then God told the angels to go forth and make heaven their home. So, the angels got up and started making themselves home in the rooms and sections in heaven. As the angel would walk into the room, the room being alive will transform itself into comfort according to the individual angel. Now imagine rooms separated but yet there are no walls. For example, let's say I walked in the room thinking about the peace and splendor of the garden of Eden. As I would walk forward into the room it will become the garden of Eden in every form. Or will be in the garden of Eden. Let's say I'm going into another room and thinking how I would like to walk on the rings of Saturn. I would be on the rings of Saturn. That is the power and speed of the angel's travel and the ability to maneuver up and down thru the three plains at thought. So, at that time all rooms were transformed according to each angel's love for God. They didn't know anything else because nothing else was created yet. Anyway, the angels kept in company of each other and always in ecstasy close to Gods throne. This was so until the Lord created the second plain or the spirit realm. That is where you'll find purgatory and the trials now. That is where the cleansing occurs before you enter the kingdom of heaven. Anyway. When the gate on the west wall was opened, and it is the same gate the Saint Peter holds the keys for and controls the entrance in and out of the kingdom of God now and forever. Saint Peter doesn't stand guard at the gate, the angels that report to Saint Peter stand guard and control the flow and answer to Saint Peter directly. You will not be stopped at the gate for all who enter in and out must be angels or accompanied by angels. That is why once a person dies in this world he will never come back to this world. The gate is closed. No angel will accompany you to come back nor allow you for this is Gods strict commandment. Only God, Jesus the Christ of God who is God and The Holy Spirit who is also God can. It even takes special permission from God for the angels to come down to the third plain or make themselves known to man in a physical form. Only for a specific reason and doing Gods bidding. That's it. So even though the guardian angels are around us, we can't see or hear them. They are not allowed to make themselves physically known. Yet they do all the work behind the scenes. Not for any glory only to be pleasing to God for His great love for them and their great love for Him. For even if it was possible, you would be like the fallen angels that were thrown out of heaven and became demons dark in color because they fell from glory and the light of eternal life diminished from within because of their distance from God and His eternal love. Now what about the ones that are brought into heaven or servants of God. That's different. First, they are always accompanied by angels and second their physical vessel or form, there body is still alive. In that case you can be accompanied into heaven but again under Gods will and commandment only. So yes, you can be going towards the light but you are accompanied by angels your spirit is not alone. It is the same for those who fall to hell. You're still being accompanied but by demons or fallen angels. God chose to give you a chance to see what will happen to you if there is no change. Anyway, I'm getting off the topic. That is a whole book on to itself. Anyway, going back to lucifer. As the other angels approached him and made themselves known they idolized his splendor. They felt he was amazing and they wanted to be by his side. They wanted to be close to him. That's exactly what happened and the first clique was formed. Just like it was in high school. The smart kids with the smart, the bullies with the bullies, etc. His admirers couldn't resist his beauty and power. God gave the angels blessings and great knowledge of almost all things that got created. However, God never gave them the power to see the future. One other blessing God gave them was the ability to move throughout the plains also the ability to understand all of the things of creation. You see, diamonds, rubies, precious stones, gold, silver, platinum and so many other. So much more than we have available on earth, decorate heaven from the beginning. There are also the heavenly hosts and beings not just the angels. God created the angels as servants to The Holy Trinity and servants of man. We are getting ahead of ourselves. Back to Lucifer. As the angels admired his beauty his knowledge his splendor, they also feared his power. Lucifer's stature was a lot greater than there's and he had other gifts they did not possess. For example, lucifer is a shift changer. He can appear to you as any human being you might know. He can possess animals or enter into anything created by God that is away from God. He can be an angel of light looking pure and innocent with a face and hair of someone you know or like a baby or a female and or male. He can change your surroundings and place you in an illusion. He is like a lion circling you whispering manipulating speaking thru you putting thoughts in you training you to unwillingly serve him by doing his bidding. The further you are from Christ the easier is the manipulation. Even unto forcing you to suicide by whispering the thoughts. If you know the devil you can fight him and expose him with the word of God and then conquer him. But first you must know God and think like God before you have the power and the knowledge to know the devil and defeat him. To do so, you must be one with Christ. When you are one with Christ and truly love Him, and repent you are cleansed and forgiven and The Holy Spirit comes like the wind and baptizes you with the fire of life and fills you with truth and love and knowledge. When God lays His Holy Spirit upon you. Then you may ask for the gifts of The Holy Spirit. With God's blessing then you are as the Saints or the Apostles full

of the fruit and gifts of the Holy Spirit. You are then attached
to God and His Holy Spirit. You then become one with God
and communication is with thought and word but it
becomes a direct and immediate line to God. Where you
say Father, I thirst and water is given. Or father heal the sick
man in your Holy name Jesus and the man is healed. You
are in direct communication with God and your senses are
occupied with heaven. You will see the angels going up and
down on our Lord Jesus. You see the angels and heavenly
hosts. You see that which is invisible which is the real reality
and this illusion we call life becomes nothing more than it
is, a temporary illusion and ground of testing and purification
of the blood lines. Life is very simple. The meaning of life is
to gain eternal life. You do so by using your free will and
choosing God or the devil. Good or bad. The constant
challenge within, of good and your own evil. Man has been
given an imperfection. That imperfection is the flesh with
the seed of death and knowledge of what is good and what
is evil. Imagine a world where you didn't know if what you
did was good or bad? Then you can't be guilty of anything
and are innocent of all things as Adam and Eve were before
they ate of the tree of knowledge. In that moment, the seed
of what is good and what is evil took root in the flesh and
affected all flesh from that moment on. You see, knowledge
is what made the pure and innocent into the guilty and
sinful. The law was written within and your actions
condemned you or set you free. All done with free will. As
the mention of man in heaven cleansed heaven of lucifer and
his followers so does lucifer and his followers cleanse man
of who will go to heaven and who will not. Then your left
at the end after the day of Judgement, with a whole creation

and family of God, that wants to be there and truly loves God with their free will. That is why the devil and his demons still exist now. They are a sifter that separates man who loves and wants God and man that serves and wants the devil. So, until that great and just day of judgement, no one dies the second death. That is why the devil and his followers still exist. God can easily speak them out of existence. God can do anything and everything. God has no limitations what's so ever. That is why we need to pray for faith.

Faith is the foundation of all things. Faith, hope and love. This is the secret. This is the formula that produces true repentance. Repentance then becomes the path that leads to your union with The Holy Trinity and eternal life consumed in eternal love. Out of the three the most important is love. So even though faith is the foundation, without love the foundation will not be solid. Upon that foundation all things are built. Including patience, forgiveness, understanding, strength, belief, care, compassion and peace. It's a matter of letting go and surrender to God after, that leads to true happiness that comes from The Holy Spirit as it fills your heart and soul with Gods love. Anyway, the angels fitted in to their surroundings in heaven and witnessed the birth of glory and radiance in heaven. Heaven alive with every breath of God was constantly transforming into Gods will as it is alive and God is always working. Lucifer wondered thru out heaven witnessing the splendor of that which the Creator has given al them. He was jealous of the splendor and wasn't comfortable with the beauty and light that was filling all the angels. He thought to himself how he can rule and sit on Gods thrown if he can only have the angels follow him. He then would be able to take heaven by force. How am I to do this he thought to himself. He watched the angels going in and out of the halls of heavenly life and called out to a group of them. They approached him in respect and he said to them that he is in charge of the angels and Gods army so they should bow to him and never resist him. He told them to witness his power and splendor as he transformed himself into creatures of heaven as a copycat and grew in stature as he flexed his splendor upon them and commanded they kneel before him. A lot of the angels turned away and said we kneel before the creator only and laughed as they hovered away but some stayed and kneeled. Behold said lucifer you being the first to kneel before my power will be made my generals and all others will kneel before you. We shall rule heaven together and sit on the thrown of power. All will show respect and fear when they are before us and heaven will be taken by force. What would you like us to do they replied? Go and recruit. Bring me my soldiers. Tell them I hold the power of life but also of death. I want to show them this gift and give it to them. They will become more powerful than the rest of the angels. But wont God destroy us said lucifer's generals? No do not fear. God has set the day for all creation to be judged. Until that day he won't kill any of us nor will he take away are gifts because we will be judged on the use of those gifts given. They have nothing to lose only to gain if they follow me. I shall give them the power to fight and to take life. When the angels heard that he has the power to take life the angels felt fear for the very first time. Under the fear they went forward and started serving Lucifer blindly. Lucifer never explained to them how they can kill their brothers he just said he can and he was willing to teach this information to his loyal followers starting with his generals. Remember Lucifer thrives on fear, lies and deceit. As lucifers' generals went out and started recruiting or trying to convince angels to join lucifer for his thirst of power of the Gods throne. They spread the roomer around that lucifer can kill them and he knows how. In other words, they started spreading fear into heaven that if you don't join him you will die or be killed. You see lucifer was a liar a thief and a murderer from the very beginning. He had all the splendor and light on the outside but inside he was getting dark like and empty shell. The more he willed against God the darker and emptier he became. All the angels were given special gifts and knowledge and to know all things upon the moment of creation. Lucifer's powers were even greater because he was to be there superior and Gods Top General. According to the rules of creation anything can die as it has lived. There is a beginning and an end. The Alpha and the Omega. As a child's birth into this world is the child's death, death in this world is the birth of eternal life in Christ. All things must die in order to live because without death there is no life. An angel dies as it surrenders its free will to God before His thrown in love and loyalty forever. Then there is a great celebration in heaven because that angel is reborn into the light and not just the flame it walked out of. That eternal light then fills the angel and he is a sun to himself but becomes a child of God and will serve in truth and eternal love and loyalty to God forever. The angel that goes against God, loses its light and turns dark as it is withdrawn from God and eternal life. This angel will then be judged on the day of judgment and be thrown back into the flame that birthed them. Then the angel will be no more. But if the angels have love, great devotion with no rebellion and a great will for Gods plan, it is not possible for any angel to die. God will bless them more because there free will has eternally been offered to God. After the day of judgement, the angels will be transformed as a new born. Born again as children of pure love and light. This is an eternal angel. There is no weakness. Anyway, God gave the angels this knowledge because He knew what lucifer was up to, and didn't want a false sense of fear to consume the angels or force them in a position they shouldn't be in from the beginning. Now that the knowledge has been spread angels started to line up for their rebirth and surrender to The Holy Trinity. The angels are unlimited. Some of course followed lucifer anyway and so the rebellion in heaven just begun. There is no time in heaven so there's is no way of determining how long or length of time after the beginning of creation or the length of anything because it doesn't exist. Days are eternal light is everywhere darkness doesn't exist. God is always working and heaven is always changing according to the needs of those who occupy it. As the angels were lining up and offering their greatest gift in their possession to God as a show of love and faith, they were being baptized in the eternal God. The love, life, knowledge of most things, mercy, care and power of God filled them thru and thru. Yet others chose to see what lucifer had to offer and flocked to his splendor. Lucifer gathered them all up for a meeting in a room in heaven where he was to discuss his plan to take heaven by force. They all gathered and they were many. Even lucifer was surprised at the power of fear. It looks like fear is respected more than love he thought to himself. Then let me be fearful he thought from this day forward. He started speaking in the tongue of angels and telling the rest of the angels gathered there lies about all the things he will do for them as a politician would and all that he offers. He made himself sound like he is god and that the true and only creator is nothing but an old weak being who has nothing but love and care to offer. To lucifer this seemed as a weakness. I am telling you the truth! It takes greater power to love and be merciful then to hate and be destructive. Love leads to life and hate leads to the 2 deaths. Lucifer with all his splendor and Godly gifts he still betrayed God. The seven deadly sins were in him. The more he moved from God, the darker and uglier he became. He who glowed brighter than the sun started to lose his light. He spoke to his followers. He spoke of power and kingdom rule. He did not want God destroyed because he knows he is eternal, but wanted instead, that God will kneel to him and his rule. Why don't you choose to serve Him asked another who was at the meeting? I will and am serving Him said lucifer. I will wait and watch and when the moment comes I shall strike. Let us know go around and see heaven and what The Lord is creating. They all agreed and hovered off seeking the corners of heaven and the end. However, there is no beginning and no end in heaven. Heaven is constant, alive and multiplying constantly. There is no ceiling and no floor. There are no walls it just seems as there are. If you walk into a hall a room prepared by the Lord you will feel like you're in a private room with walls yet the room has no beginning and no end. No floor or ceiling. Depending of what you seek you shall find in the room accordingly to your free will. I walked into a room seeking Saint John the Baptist. I found

Saint John and a gold waterfall where he baptized me and gave me to drink of the water of heaven. It is like that. I went into a room and met with the apostles sitting on thrones, each as bright as a sun. In another room there was The Virgin Mary in peace with floors and what seemed to be a garden with a water fall. The floors are not as the ones of this world. They were so colorful and the scents were all in unison with each other in total visual and harmonies perfection. In another room I found Moses and Elijah. I walked outside the halls of the kingdom and saw David with his crown of glory speaking with Solomon who wore his own crown. Before Gods throne raising up from what seemed to be the floor were the prayers of repentance. Like incense. The Holy Trinity excepting the prayers and heaven celebrating. Anyway, let's get back to Lucifer. He went back and his followers behind him spread across heaven Their formation was one of a dragon and lucifer was the head. As his face shifted from side to side he seemed as if he had three heads. The three heads of lucifer represent his three faces. One as an angel of light. One as the angel of murder and betrayal and one as the angel of lies and deception. The head or the face of the angel of light is the betrayer. Christ had Judas. God had lucifer. The Holy Spirit has man.

But be warned: God can forgive all things if repentance is true and from the heart. But if you blaspheme The Holy Spirit which is life and pure love, there is NO forgiveness! That is exactly what the devil has done continuously.

Anyway, lucifer went back to the room of thrones and saw God wasn't there. He made his way to the throne and the throne roared at him, it seemed to be lion heads burst forth from the throne and the eagle on the top of the throne shrieked. The heavenly hosts witnessed and warned to stay away from their creator's throne in the heavenly language. God was in another section of heaven knowing what lucifer is up to and with the knowledge of all things. Still God gave lucifer a chance to repent. You see, God loves us all. People ask, why does the Lord allow the bad to exist and the good he takes and they die young in this world? If you accept that we are here to get into heaven than the faster you are acceptable to God the faster you get in. Unless you are given a gift or you need to be here for a specific service. When your time or service is up, you are then called home. An atheist would be given a long life as would many on the path of evil. They are given more time to seek and find the truth who is The Holy Trinity. Imagine you had children. One was good and you gave all things too. One is bad and murders. You gave him everything as well but he is rebellious and betrayal lives in his heart. Then as a parent you love and feel pain for both. Imagine God says to you ok now my child pick from your 2 kids who goes to heaven and who dies the two deaths and ends up in hell. God loves us so much, that He wishes none to perish. The Holy Trinity gives time hoping we come to our senses and repent and as a wondering black sheep, for us to find our way and return to the flock. A lot of times The Holy Spirit will send helpers to guide you. When that happens and it does, when the prodigal son returns there is great cause for celebration in heaven. For the prodigal son walked the path of light and walked the path of the tempting darkness and chose with his or her free will to return once and for all to the eternal path of God and light. Those are usually the servants of God who are the most productive for the kingdom of heaven and The Holy Trinity. Yes, some are lost or completely consumed by the devil. However, they will always have plenty of chances to repent. God is good always and fair. Even if Judas, would have returned to the cross and asked for forgiveness in true repentance, God would have forgiven the betrayal as He forgave Saint Peter for his denial. However, because Judas hid a part of his heart and was struck by grief, the devil filled hi with sorrow, anger and grief enough to bring him to take his own life. These are all gifts from the devil. The further you are from God, the more vulnerable you are to demonic temptation. Ask yourself every morning, whom am I serving today God? Or the devil? The tree is known by its fruit. Whom we belong too is known from our actions and not from our words. Well, as God was working and preparing rooms in heaven with His word who is Christ, lucifer was preparing heaven with rebellion. Lucifer loved God and God loves the whole of His creation even though most of His creation is upsetting to God. God is perfect and great. Only The Holy Trinity is perfection. So sinful ways with no repentance and rejoicing in lies and deceit is offensive to God. The seven sins and vanity are paths to death and damnation. I still can't believe that in today's times, people still practice the ways of the devil in a great degree. Did you know that the satanic bible is one of the best sellers in the world? Remember it is secrets that were revealed to man by fallen angels that have caused man, death and suffering. It all started with the fruit of knowledge of good and evil. If you commit sin and you do not know it is sin, then how can it be held against you by God? But once you find out that it is evil or bad and you willingly repeat the sin without remorse or repentance, then the sin is held against you as your soul is scared with the sin. Thank God, He gave us His Beloved Son Jesus so that we can be saved. On our own merits it's virtually impossible to be eternal and live. Abraham loves his son. Yet when the Lord asked him to sacrifice the son he waited so long for and that he loves so much Abraham respond and brought his son up to the alter to sacrifice him to God. Abraham remained and proved that Gods will first and then everything else. In return for his faith love and loyalty, not only did Isaac not die under his father's knife but he birthed forth a new nation. God seeing Abrahams loyalty and love, blessed him and called him righteous. Through Abraham a nation of followers in The Holy Trinity emerged. What a bloodline to be part of? Then God in return knowing man on his own merits can't come before His purity and not die, sent His Son for sacrifice for man's salvation. After Abraham past the test for man God delivers His word in the flesh as a true innocent and pure unblemished sacrifice Jesus. If you have faith and believe you are then saved. The body and blood of Christ is eternal. When thru faith it is consumed and a part of you, well you become eternal as well and belong to the body of Christ. When Jesus was nailed to the cross above his head was a sign that read the king of the Jews. It was written in three languages. Why? Everything done was God's plan and is God's plan. The different languages represent the different people and blood lines that the Lord was crucified for. Isn't that interesting. It is those who will become his body. It was Gods way of getting these people or us Christians into the kingdom of heaven and eternal life, thru faith and repentance alone. Let my son pay for your sins sayth the Lord. In return Love Him, have faith in Him, believe in Him and just ask for forgiveness. If you do not have Christ, I am sorry to say, you are and will be under Gods wrath. Who will save you on the day of judgement as you stand before the perfect Holy Trinity? Will your scared sinful soul be able to withstand purity and perfection? Is pure and unblemished light. Your soul can disintegrate and be consumed easily by Gods power. Look what happened to Moses. He serves God but did not have Christ. His sins remained scares on his soul. So, when Moses asked to look upon Gods face, God said he could not. He would not survive. The Lord allowed him to witness God from behind as he walked by him. Even then Moses aged and shriveled up like a prune. He became old and white with shriveled up skin. His hair his beard all turned white. He went from middle aged to looking like a very old man. You see? Without Jesus our Lord and God, we would never be able to survive Gods presence, our body and soul will disintegrate instantly because of our imperfections. God created us perfect and good. Our free will and the knowledge of good and evil, has turned us into sinners, has blanket us with imperfection and lead us to death. God knowing this sent us Christ whose blood washes away imperfection and sin and His body which is eternal makes us eternal upon faith, belief and consumption. Once the eternal blood and flesh of Christ is consumed thru faith by Christians then we too are cleansed and healed. We then are perfect and eternal in The Lord. We then receive a place in Gods table and we become part of the inner circle of Gods kingdom. The greater your faith, your love, your belief, your repentance and sacrifice, the closer you will be to God for all eternity. To him that overcomes, I will share my throne sayth The Lord. All for the sake of love and to be pleasing to our Heavenly Father. Its obedience. To give up sin is surrender. Both are required for righteousness. Not for the praise of man but for the blessings of God. Anything against Gods word and love is pure rebellion. Rebellion against Gods word leads to a path of destruction. When you serve the devil, don't expect anything good but death at the end of your journey. As lucifer continued his recruiting God was busy multiplying all things in heaven. The rooms were being prepared for all who were to come. There was the creation of the room of souls. The Lord gathered Michael, Uriel, Raphael and Gabriel and said to them come and follow me. I have something to show just to the four of you. The lord entered into a room and commanded a gold basin decorated full of all the rubies, diamonds, all types of precious stones and gold to appear in all splendor and glory. It was very large and then the Lord commanded this basin which looked like a round swimming pool seven feet by seven feet wide and seven feet deep to be filled with what seemed to be a thick liquid. He then turned to His angels and said this Holy room will remain sealed and guarded. Michael place two other guardian angels one on each side of the door both with a 2-edged flaming sword. No one is to be allowed to enter this room. Michael, Gabriel, Raphael and Uriel, prepare your brothers and tell them to be aware. For what Lord? The angels asked. Even now the enemy is preparing to take my throne by force explained The Lord. When Lord will the enemy strike? Not yet said The Lord but very soon. Now there is still question in the enemies will about serving Me or serving himself. There is still the chance of repentance.

There are those who plot against me. Why not just destroy them Lord? You are the giver of all life and the taker away there of? My blessings and gifts are eternal. There will be the time of judgement for all I have created according to their actions led by their free will. There will be a time when I will ask of each the return of the gifts I have given. What was done with them will either condemn or exalt the holder of my talents. Yes, Father as you will. Michael went and called 3 guardians angels and brought them before the Lord. The Lord blessed them and great power came upon them from The Holy Spirit. They grew in stature and glowed. The two-edged flaming swords came forth from God and the angels accepted each one. As they accepted the sword it joined there being and became one with them. They each took place one on each side of the room of souls as God commanded. Not because they had too, but because they wanted to for the great love they have for The Holy Trinity. Then God walked alone to the gold basin as the other angels waited outside. Come forth The Lord Creator said to me. I approached cautiously towards God. Then the Lord said be NOT afraid. Come and see. As I approached God started to shape in the form of a man yet beautifully perfected. He smiled and was brighter than 100 suns. There was lightning and thunder coming from his eyes and He seemed as if he had a body made of fine polished brass with long beautiful white hair and beard yet so young looking at the same time without a wrinkle on His perfected skin. I was about to ask the Lord creator if that is His natural form, Yet God which is The Holy Trinity answered me before the words left my mouth and said. I AM The ALMIGHTY! I AM The Alpha and OMEGA! I AM and always have been and will be!

There is no other but Us in three as in one we are for I Am. At that moment I witnessed the words that God was speaking come to life and started to take the form of God but in a younger version. Younger meaning without the white hair and beard yet all the other features were exactly alike. The Lords hair was like fine gold strands mixed with other brownish colors they were like a combination of all the colors yet the hair was dark and light at the same time. The holy Spirit was like in the shape of a dove but large in stature with a face of the most beautiful angel and childlike features in pure innocence and perfection. We are I AM! And as God said that behold I heard heaven shake and thunder. My Son who is I and my Holy Spirit. Behold My Spirit which is Holy, pure and never-ending love. I witnessed The Holy Trinity as Three as they separated into 3 different beings and were around the pool of souls. He will be in our image and we shall call him man they all were in constant agreement. Come forth replacer of lucifer and stand by my side. I walked towards God and saw the Holy trinity smiling at me. Yet in my heart I knew I wasn't worthy and that I am a sinful man. I started to weep. God said with a thundering voice. There are none who are worthy but are deemed righteous by my blood and are chosen. I went close to God and great peace and love blanketed me and filled me. Behold my love in my perfection. As The Holy Trinity said these words in unison as if rehearsed to say it perfectly at the same time, God then breathed into the basin and the basin was filled full of souls. It is finished they replied as the room of souls was now complete. The souls were alive in the basin moving around yet they were white in color without shape or bodies or faces. They looked like little baby angels.

Timothy! Yes, Lord I replied in ecstasy and awe. As I AM three and yet one so shall man be three and yet one. Only if they Have my Holy Spirit. If they do not, thru faith, have my Son, whom I have sacrificed for my creations, then they will not have me in completion. Thru my Son who is I, there is forgiveness for their sins. Without my Son they will not have pure forgiveness nor will they have my Holy Spirit. The day of judgement has just begun. The Lord spoke and said behold my yolk is comforting and soothing. I will wipe away sin from the hearts of man and purify and heal the scars on their souls caused by sin. As I give perfection the soul of man can't be returned to I with imperfections. For that reason, I AM and sin, death and all imperfection that comes forth from free will be wiped clean thru my blood and flesh sayth the Lord. All who eat my flesh and drink my blood will become eternal in my kingdom. For my flesh is the real food and my blood the real drink and is eternal. Only if you believe in Me. Will you have me thundered The Holy Spirit and if you believe and love Us said The Lord and The Holy Spirit, you will be one with me, said God with a voice of a pure and innocent child. I love you with all my heart, soul and spirit my God, as I wept and cried tears of joy while in peace and ecstasy. I know you from the beginning timothy God said. I know you never felt nor will there ever exist a greater love for you to experience or have experienced than I. I see your love burning uncontrollably as an untamed fire burning you thru and thru. That is why you have been chosen from the beginning. Gather on to me my scattered flock. The day of judgement is close at hand. Deliver on to me my souls given to man so that they may be purified by my Son. When purified, I can welcome them to my table in their new eternal bodies. How will my body look I asked? I continued by asking, will it be fat for I battled with weight all my life so far. The Lord smiled and said. You will be the first of my new creation for you will be man and angel. Your body, your blessings and power will be like no other, for you will stand by our side eternally. The place once made for lucifer will now be yours. It will be you who will throw him into the eternal flame as he is consumed on the day I judge all of creation by my eternal flame of creation. There will be no other as you. I thank the Lord and for the first time I felt like a child of God worthy pure and innocent. I was used to feeling guilty and sinful full of shame to even raise my eyes to heaven. Yet now, I was looking and speaking to God. I have been made acceptable to God thru my Lord whom I believe in and have consumed. Who in fact is God himself. His word that became flesh. The lamb of God His sacrifice for man. Eat my flesh drink my blood and you will live. Making us who are imperfect, perfect thru himself. There is no greater love than Gods love for us. God tested man thru Abraham and asked him to sacrifice Isaac. As Abraham raised the sword to sacrifice Isaac God stopped him and man past the test thru Abraham. God seeing that man loves Him, He instead did that for man which Abraham was going to do for God. He sacrificed His Son Jesus who is God. Just like Isaac is a son of Abraham. It's so beautiful when you think about it. There is a time offsetting that we all go thru in this life by God. When we get thru it we are then rewarded with blessings from God for this world and Heaven. God tests us because we possess free will. It is free will and actions that make us creators as well. It all comes to life with our word. We speak into creation our destiny.

God then called out to Michael, Gabriel, Raphael and Uriel. Yes, Father? the angels replied. Take my child down to the pit and let him observe the wickedness of the fallen ones. Let him witness that which awaits all who chose to serve the created instead of the creator. Father? Show him the seven levels of hell that is in the core of the earth? Asked the angels at the same time. Yes, replied the Lord. Stay with him and watch over him. Explain to him all that I have explained to you and all you have witnessed and heard. Timothy, fear not for my Spirit is upon you. Father are we to go without being witnessed. No, I want all the demons and him who betrayed me to see my child and to know him. Let them fear him and wonder about him. Go, and let him observe the seven levels of hell and the final transformation of death. Yes, Lord replied the angels. Come servant of the most high, let us go and witness the house of the dragon where the serpent dwells in his destruction. The angels surrounded me and we walked together. As we were walking the floor of heaven seemed to open and I witnessed a round shaped cone in the middle of nowhere. It looked like those ice cream cones with the point at the end. However, there was no beginning and no end and nothing around the cone. It occupied my full vision as I watched dragon looking creatures with more than one head, circulating around the top where the entrance to hell is. We approached the demons yet we were no longer walking but it seemed as flying towards the entrance. I felt the angels holding me and we swiftly came before the entrance. Serpents behold I await the day to annihilate you and throw you into the unquenchable pit. You were given a chance to repent cried Michael and instead you have become worse and brought even more destruction. The three angels thundered their voices at the same time and said? It was the Lords will to spare you, left to us and we would have destroyed you outside the gates of heaven. The demons trembled at the site of the three angels when all of the sudden from the bottom of the pit came upwards what seemed in lightning fast speed this huge dragon looking creature with three heads. How dare you come to my kingdom said satan to the angels. He immediately slithered towards me in a flash and approached me. The devil then looked me up and down like a beast sniffing me at the same time as a lion ready to tear and consume its pray. Why are you not afraid in your sinful flesh? The devil asked. I fear The Lord our God creator of all things visible and invisible, I said. I do not fear the created. He stunk of sulfur and burnt oil. But with Gods spirit upon me I was not afraid and at peace. Actually, I felt very powerful. Like if I commanded with my voice hell would shake and crumble into itself. He jumped on me to tear my flesh as I heard screaming and tearing of souls beneath him. Red was the surrounding with burning flames and souls being tortured. As he tried to touch me he was shocked as if he touched lightning and Gods Holy Spirit thru satan so far down in a second that he had to fly right back up to me from the bottom of the pit again. All the demons were now shocked and moved back away from us. Satan came and approached Michael. Who is he? why are you here? It is our Lords will that he witnesses the false kingdom you call yours. These souls are mine in here, you can't have them. They have served me and done my will on the face of the earth. Even now as they go thru the different levels of torture and their light is permanently distinguished, they will be transformed into my demonic soldiers and will be mine to rule. They will soar up from the bottomless pit in pure darkness, transformed into my dark army with no life or light remaining within them that is of God. Serpent! roared Michael, you are pure evil, how dare you think, that they, or anyone else can save you from Gods wrath on the day of judgement. If it wasn't for our Fathers mercy, patience and love, I would have already ended you long ago. As Michael finished speaking Raphael transformed with the blazing sword and in his glorious armor and went to leap upon the devil yet Michael said let him be for now brother it is not yet his time nor our Fathers' will. Even he has work to finish as he separates the good from the evil. Uriel turned to me and explained that as the news of the creation of man rung thru heaven and cleansed heaven from the good angels and those who will fall, so does the fallen ones sift man from he who will live life eternal in heaven and he who will die alongside the fallen ones. At the end there will be a heavenly kingdom, one in perfection with only those who deserve to be there and as a family we will be one with God blanketed with His love. Even you serpent, have your use and that is the reason it is not your time yet. Gabriel turned to the devil and said if it wasn't for Gods use of you I would have happily destroyed you. Michael then commanded the devil to move aside as we entered the first circular level of hell. Behold Michael said, notice those souls who are being torn as if they were flesh. There was screaming and gnashing of teeth sounds of torture and death whaling and cursing. Howling and tearing. I watched a soul being tortured as it was torn with big cuts bathing in fire and the screaming, the smell of burnt oil and sulfur everywhere. Brothers? Why are they being tortured like that? I asked.

Their souls are being torn and shredded with big gashes that heal so they can be tortured again and again. Michael replied that this is the first level where all who enter will pay for their torturing of others on earth. The more you caused people on earth to suffer and caused them harm the more you will suffer. Behold the soul of hitler, who even at this moment is still in the first level of suffering and continuous torture. Here you find all the evil beings who done harm to man and have turned against God suffering until the day our Father judges all creation. How many levels are there and why? I asked? Each level needs to be passed all the way to the bottom where the demon layer exists. All will go thru the seven levels of suffering and then at the bottom the transformation has occurred where the soul no longer carries any light of the creator. We will take you thru all the levels and show you the devils' layer and his army. You will not write all you see replied all 4 angels at the same time. It is Gods will for you to write a separate book one of the seven you are to write. What do you mean I replied? There will be seven books as God willed. One will be a book about what you witness in hell and what you hear. Now you will just give a brief description of what you see. Later it will be one of great detail. We will take you to the past, present and future of hell as you witness the secrets of the devil and his followers. It is time, and the Lords will, that all that is done and has been done in secretive darkness by the devil, will finally be brought out into the light thru you. I know it seems as a very hard task replied Raphael blessed one, however continued Michael, these seven books shall bring people to repentance and souls will be forgiven and saved. The glory is always Gods and the praise, yes answered

Gabriel, and you have accepted the will of The Lord. Be not afraid said Uriel, we are now always with you. The seven books are man's call to Christ. The time is coming, the preparations have been done. Gods judgement is upon the earth. Send these books out as the final warning. What will the other books be about I asked? We do not know to answer replied all four angels in unison. That is for God to show you and for the Holy Spirit to teach you. Turn and witness as we go thru all the realms. No need to write all will be written within you and recalled at the proper time for others as this is their final warning. Behold the ones who murdered and killed violently the innocent. See how the demons are on top of them ripping their eyes out biting their ears of. Notice how they try to run and hide deaf and blind and see the flying creatures as they eat out their tongues as they are whipped by their demon captives. What are the others over there across the realm. What is that thing. It is satan who is a shape shifter that has transformed into the creature you see with razor sharp teeth. He is massive I replied. Don't be alarmed it's one of his forms as he shapes shifts. He is still the rotten, murdering liar, betrayer and love hater he was from the beginning. What is he doing? He is picking up the souls as you would pick up a person from his head with a body and he is chewing on them as they scream in torcher. They are gushing out worms and scum and thick puss liquid and what is that as it seems to be like blood. Satan will chew on the bones of all the dead who serve him as he tries to consume the light that is still left in their soul which was given to all by God and he's eating their free will. As long as a flicker of light exists they can still repent and be saved. If they turn over the light and free will and the demon consumes them, then they are transformed into a demon and on the day of judgement they will die the second death. But as long as they take the suffering and don't give up, there is still a chance for them. How I asked? This is not for you to write now, save it for the book of hell and redemption where you will go in great detail of what was, what is and what shall be for the devil and his followers. Look over there I cried what are those things what are they doing? Oh my God! They are eating the babies of the woman. Uriel replied. Those women, will stay there reliving the birth and suffering the pain of all those abortions one thousand times seventy-seven time. What? I cried those women aborted willfully their children so satan sits there and eats them as they give birth to them over and over again while they watch. They go thru the suffering and pain of labor and then the demon snatches the child and eats it in front of them. Again, and again. He even sucks and tears their umbilical cord and placenta right out of them. Raphael, Michael, Gabriel, Uriel, brothers, you mean that if a woman had an abortion she will suffer such a fate until the day of judgement? Not all replied the angels. Those who were raped, those who lost their children before birth those who truly repented and ask for forgiveness in truth the Lord will show mercy and they will not. Those who have murdered the innocent and have not repented will die. As their unborn died. How can he chew them like that and spit them out? Don't worry the children born have no soul and are nothing but flesh or dirt. It is the pain of the birth, the ripping if the umbilical cord and placenta and the viewing the child being killed and eaten, that is the torcher for those who have killed the innocent. You see the bugs the lizards the scorpions and the snakes going in and out of their bodies? there tearing into their souls and chewing on the breasts as they eat them from the inside out. As that is happening they are watching their child eaten. But it is really not a child but dirt. What about the woman that unknowingly had intercourse with demons or the demonically possessed? The same applies said Gabriel. There were angels of a time times 7 ago that had fallen as well. Willfully they came to earth and gave up their birth rights. They were to watch and protect but instead they possessed and raped, mutilated and ripped the innocence out of God's creation. We shall see them all bounded in another layer. They are no longer allowed to travel between the plains but wait bounded in the bottom of the pit. They saw the woman and men and they came down and possess them so they can have their ways with them. We have not been created as male or female by our Father replied Michael. As the watchers observed the man and woman in love having a child they became jealous that they could not. They gave up their rights and possessed man and had relations with each other. While doing so the innocent woman gave birth to giants. What happened to these giants. All the fallen are incapable of any good. They are evil. Anything evil births forward evil. They all had to die a violent death. The angel of death and the four horsemen traveled the earth and cleaned up the mess. As we gathered the them one by one and bounded them to the pit of hell. Now they are there awaiting judgement. You shall see them soon. Behold the other realm. Look there said Uriel. What do you see? As we suddenly appeared in another area in the cone of hell which has the shape of a tornado. Who are those spirits walking backwards and why are those flying beasts that look like those flying dinosaurs as they are called on earth eating their brains and tongues. Not only said Raphael. Look closer brother, as I looked closer I saw them. They had no eyes the flying beasts were eating their brains one little peace at a time their heads were twisted backwards and their tongues were pierced and pulled all the way down their necks where the beasts would peck and eat them as they painfully walked around in circles having nowhere to go. They were mocked and yelled at by other beast like flying creatures as they swooped down on them and tore their souls with their long nail like paws. I saw their souls ripping as it was flesh. I heard the language those beasts spoken and I understood. They kept calling to all of them behold who is it who hurts you false profit. Who will bite you next? Look into your future. Who shall tear your soul into shreds? Who are all those people I asked as I witnessed all the suffering. Michael replied, they are the fortune tellers, the false profits, the witches and their crystal balls, the tarot card users and the Ouija boards. Those using black magic or white or any other type and the false religious practices. Like which I asked? all the practices that are not of God. There is no good magic. It is all evil from the devil. Human beings are tricked and fooled. Especially from the things they see. He, the devil knows where to place his head demons as he possesses the appropriate that will have the greatest following. After all it is a battle of souls. Then the sheep just follow all the way to the slaughter. That's how tricky and sneaky he is. The devils only plan is to kill man before he gets a chance to turn to Christ and repent. Forgiveness, mercy, faith, hope and love in true repentance is the only way to God's grace. That is thru Jesus The Christ alone. In our Lord there is salvation and forgiveness of sin. Gods judgement passes over you and you are cleansed by the Lord's blood as you consume both flesh and blood in faith. Man is to be baptized in the name of The Father, The Son and The Holy Spirit. Look over there said Michael. What do you see? I see fire and liquid flame being poured on those there. Who are they? There you find the atheist, the non-believers, the antichrists and all who practice all their false rituals believing that they are worthy of salvation because in their minds have done what they considered to be good. They are being baptized with burning lava and fire and they are being burned as if they had flesh. What are those creatures dancing around and circulating around and on top of those down further? Come said the angels as they took me down further to the pit. Brothers I replied can we go all the way to the bottom so that I might witness the birth or transformation of soul to demon? We are said Gabriel however you are not to write about that mystery until another time. Yes, I replied. As we approached I saw souls in form of flesh with demons on top of them others kept vomiting and were being forced to vomit and others had demons on their back causing them to continuously be bent over. Others seemed like the demons were having sexual intercourse with them male on male and female on female with serpent tongues and burning sulfur. They screamed in pain as if they were newborns babies and whaled. They try to get away but the demons were constantly on their backs forcing themselves to enter into the soul thru the rectum of men and women and then the demon will grow in size and rip the souls from the inside out as their bodies would tear in half and after all the pain and screaming they would be thrown into fire where they would burn and heal so that they may relive it again and again. They take their sharp bear like claws and dig into what seems to be the neck and repeat the actions as screams of crying children are heard everywhere. These things we are showing you are things of mystery and secret. This is a world created by the devil to serve his needs and his followers pay the price. This is not Gods will but those souls that have surrendered to anything or anyone but The Holy Trinity must pass thru here and face him that they served willingly or without knowing. But the Apostle Paul said that he who is without knowledge that what he commits is sin is forgiven and not held against them. Yes, replied the angels. We are in time where all the world has heard the truth and salvation comes thru the son. It is the only way to God. Whether one admits or not it is the truth. There is no such thing as I have not heard or I do not know or have not seen. The world knows the truth. Jesus is the only Son, The Christ of God and as it has been eternally written, salvation comes thru Him alone. Everyone else must pass thru the trials before they can pass into the different levels of heaven. So, in the case let's say of a Buddhist for example who is loving caring and with no harm, what will happen to him. He will go thru the process of being purified and after he will be allowed in the outer courtyard of heaven. Those who are Christs once entered into The Kingdom, are close to God. Others who come into heaven will be allowed to be in certain areas further away from God. So, the Buddhist will be in the garden of Eden but will not know God. Even though he will hear Him. I understand I replied. So? You will explain the hierarchy of our home in another book, do not write what we explain to you now. Yes, I replied and the angels spoke. As they spoke dragons and demons were flying up from the pit. They couldn't even approach us we were like a sun all together and a great light in hell. They had souls in their mouths and people screaming and asking us to help them and rescue them. To give them water as their mouths burned of fire and sulfur. But we couldn't do anything because they were the demons' possessions for a time, times a time, times seven. Which will be the day of judgement. All things are possible with God replied the angels and all must have faith. It is never too late for salvation. Not even if you are here replied the angels. The Lord wants no one to be lost. He awaits to gather all His children and hold them to His loving bosom as a Father would hold his new born child. Come, lets us see more. Write in brief detail the rest and do not reveal all that you see but instead briefly write what is seen. You will explain at another time. God has revealed mysteries as the last call to man before judgement. Repent and save your life. As the angels guided me thru hell I saw people eating continuously until there stomachs' burst and then like dogs eating again all things that spilled out their busted stomachs' until they burst again. This cycle kept repeating. I saw wealthy and rich all who killed and stepped over bodies for their love of money being torn to bits by the demons as they were mocked. How much shall you pay me not to torcher you the demons asked? As they were fed the bones of the dead and the families they destroyed. Over and over until they would throw up maggots and bugs, spiders and scorpions as they pierced their tongues. Then this huge beast will come and gather them and eat them and chew on them as they screamed in agony. I saw the demons at the bottom of the pit preparing as they war against man and God. I saw the rapist being raped. I saw all who torcher and kill being tortured and ripped to shreds in agony and their souls being healed as scared flesh and then being tortured and ripped to shreds. The cries and begging of death. Eating and vomiting crying and burning as all the different forms of satans created would spread their torchers over all their captives. I wept as I witnessed everything and the angels surrounded me and hugged me as a peace came over me. Oh, warrior of our Father peace be with you. Do not weep over the dead but celebrate all those in heavenly light for they are alive. If it wasn't for Gods mercy, who sacrificed His only beloved Son Jesus for the sake of man's eternal life, heaven would be empty of man. All this suffering of all that you see here in the millions, is nothing compared to the suffering endured By the Christ our Lord Jesus. What do you mean I eagerly replied to the angels? When Jesus our God was in the garden before man betrayed Him, God His Father had already started to pour His suffering upon Him as The Lord sweated blood. Gods wrath that was being poured on the Lord plus man's wrath being poured on Gods flesh until His crucifixion and releasing His Spirit to His Father, was more excruciating and painful then all of hell and its suffering. These souls you see in hell if you were to gather all their pain and suffering it will still not equal to Gods wrath that was poured on His Christ. That is how much Jesus loves man. He endured His Fathers will and paid for all the generations and the blood lines sins. All man has to do is believe and have faith in Jesus Christ. He is the only way to God. It is written! Do not feel sorry for them and let the dead bury their own dead. For eternal life comes thru Christ. When the Lord was crucified the sign above His had written in the three languages represented the foundation of his children that belong to Him and their blood lines of believers. For He was crucified for those people possessing those languages and their generations to come as their blood lines are cleansed. After the angels were done explaining to me the bloodlines, Gods' voice thundered thru hell and shook everything greater than any earthquake as God commanded the angels to take me to the past where Satan first devised his plan with the rest of the fallen ones. The plan to kill all of mankind. The angels lifted me all circled me as I felt lighter than a feather and we went straight down into the pit all the way to the bottom as a vortex into an area which seemed like it was the center of the earth where all the lava and core is that keeps the earth alive. As we stepped over the burning river of fire we entered somewhere that seemed to be as a cave. There satan was speaking to his followers as they were creating their plan with the language of the fallen and the writing there of. He is the creator we are the created. How can you place your thrown above or be more powerful you who has been created than Him who created you? Satan moved his claw towards him who was speaking and grabbed the fallen one from what seemed to be his head and pulled him to his face and said. Behold my power where I can end you and since you lack faith I shall show you how to create and how much greater I am as a creator than Him who created all things. What do you mean slithered the rest of satans generals? God created man from dirt. So, shall we create a new species from dirt lava and that black liquid. We call the liquid oil. He will be greater and more powerful than man and we shall create him in our image. As satan and the fallen ones went to the river of fire, brimstone, oil, fire, lava, dirt was everywhere around them it was the center of the earth. Let us all create a new being in our image. Satan tries to copy God so he may be like God replied Michael explaining to me in detail of what is going on. The devil and the demons started forming and creating using the materials found in the core of the earth these big beasts others huge with teeth and others huge with small teeth. Others with wings and others with horns. Others were greater and others were smaller. They all created beasts that are in their image. Image they hold within. No matter how much they tried to copy man or even a dog they could not. They could only create what they had inside. Beast like creatures which man has named dinosaurs. How can we bring them to life? God breathed into man a soul. What are we to do asked satans generals? We can possess them. Well use them as vehicles and raid the earth and consume man. As the devil took charge and possessed his powerful vehicle being the most powerful dinosaur and most fierce the rest did the same. As they took this creature and possessed them they started across the river of fire which infused them together even more and made the outer skin thick and hard and started making their way up thru the different levels of the earth so that they can reach the surface. However, the lord seeing this and what they were up to, shook the earth condemned them and the dinosaurs fell to the ground lifeless even under possession. Satan screamed as he came out of his creation with wrath and anger, and so did the other demons. God cursed the dinosaurs and froze them into stone and then they broke apart into pieces. As God cursed satans creation he commanded the earth to throw up these abominations as a witness against satan and his hate for man. However, man in their so-called knowledge and all the false teaching of scientists and atheists, embraced them and display the demon's creations and even like them. Satan did this by using the faithless to stir away faith from the faithful and question all things of God. So, every time there is an earthquake or shift the earth throws up the parts and bones of their dinosaurs as a reminder to man and because the earth allowed satan to actually use her parts for his abominations. All things created by God will be judged accordingly on the day of judgement even the stone. Let's us go further down into the pit. Do not write in detail of what you see replied the angels. Instead just a brief description until the book of hell is revealed to you in fullness as it is one of the seven books you are to write. The angels encircled me as we went down further into the pi as a tornado. Behold the creature that is called vanity. Here you will find all who love vanity as the creature tears and destroys their lust. How so? I asked. Michael responded by saying, if your vanity is your beauty the demon tears your face or body again and again. According to your vanity the demons responds with giving you the opposite and the pain of suffering is such that you repeat it until judgement. Brothers, I replied. Why does the Lord allow this suffering? The Holy Trinity is loving and forgiving. Why such suffering in this place? Why is it allowed by God? God is good always! These souls that are here, do not belong to the God. They have willingly given up God for service and love for their desires and the devil. All are receiving their reward from the devil. God is all good. The devil is all bad. If you belong to God and your love is and belongs to The Holy Trinity, you then repent in truth and are forgiven. If you serve the devil which is evil in its purest form, then can you expect your reward to be good?

Since the devil is incapable of being or doing anything good? Now do you see. You belong to God; the devil can't harm you. If you belong to the devil, then God will not interfere with the path chosen by your free will, and you receive your punishment by your jailor who is the devil. God forgives. God is always good. The devil kills and is always bad. As I listened to the angels and I started witnessing the rest of the torchers that were being shown to me. I wept as it was very painful to my spirit to witness. Souls being ripped apart in agonistic pain begging me to help them to give them some drink to sooth the blisters in their mouths and on there bodies. The heat, the suffering, was so excruciating. They drank vinegar and the devil poured burning sulfur and hot lava and their open wounds. There were souls full of blisters. The demons were ripping the blisters all over their souls there tore and bled like flesh. One at a time with their sharp claws the demons tore the boils on the soul created by sin and the puss like liquid poured out of their wounds and wouldn't stop. The demons would lick and suck on their wounds and more would pour out. They looked like lepers just 1000 times worse. The blisters seemed alive and puffing up like a balloon and getting bigger and bigger until the demon would burst them and eat that which came out of there. In another section I saw souls being forced to eat worms and maggots and other disgusting creatures I have never seen on earth as those things consumed would eat them from the inside out. We went lower and as we traveled the souls and the punishment became worse and worse. The pain the screams were ringing in my ears. The suffering and the demons laughing and enjoying torching them as their souls healed over and over again and the torchers continued.

They were never ending. We went all the way down to the bottom of the pit. Behold said Michael. I laid my eyes on 3 demons that looked like dinosaurs with wings and horns on their head. One of them was bruised really bad yet had healed and seemed to be very powerful. This is the antichrist. As I approached him his eyes blood shot and death suffering and war destruction everything was revealed in his eyes. You think you can save them? Do you? He asked. I do not! I replied. I am not The Savior there is only one. The Son of God, and his name is Jesus. He must like you the tempter said. You must be special. Aren't you he hissed? No, I am nothing but a sinner who is saved by my Lord The Christ of God. Come he replied I shall give you power on the earth to serve me and all shall follow you and your number. Nations will bow to you and all treasures will be yours. You will be greater than all the kings. I will give you power to command my demons and they will serve you. Join me, I am not bad. You will be reborn unto the earth as my son and your life will start all over again. You will enjoy wealth and the things of this world. Serve me I am the real god. Many of the earths servants of God serve me. You can rule over them all. Don't you see how I'm feared even by your companions? The angels didn't reply but instead waited. I was the one having the conversation. He showed all the things I will have in my newly born life. My power. You will heal the sick and perform miracles. People will praise you as a god replied the demon. All those who will oppose you will fall dead to your feet. No one on the earth will be more powerful. I gazed into the demon's face and looked him straight in the eyes and saw Armageddon. Death famine destruction and the nations praising me as king and even calling me a god. I said to the serpent in a voice that all creation can hear. Get behind me satan! I serve the Lord my God and only Him! He screamed and grew in stature immediately and I saw his chains he was bounded down in the pit of hell. At that moment the angelic companions grew in stature and they glowed. Swords came out of them with two sharp edges and flames. They wore armor and were fierce greater than lions as they went forward and struck the demons with their swords. How dare you try to recruit Gods olive tree. Thunder wrung in hell and everything shook. Let them be! For only a short time more. Gods voice was heard my loving servant has passed his trial. Bring him back now. This is not the moment of redemption Michael. Come back with your brothers. Bring me my loving child. As the angels obeyed and holstered their swords their armor disappeared and came down inside them. They all replied at the same time by saying, "remember all you have seen, but most of all remember the secret of how to get out of hell". The knowledge given to me became one with me, as it was written inside me. The angels then surrounded me and we all flew straight up out of the pit of hell. As we were going up it seemed like the top opened and we came through what seemed to be the floor of heaven. I see all things and know all things thundered the voice of God. I am from the beginning without an end. Then the Lord asked. Where is my olive tree? I replied instantly, here I am Lord! Let it be so, that from this day forward a scripture, my word is fulfilled. You shall tell the churches and the nations I am Jesus Lord and The Christ. I am the seed and offspring of David and the bright morning star. I AM Salvation. I Am and thru Me all things are. I fell to my knees worshipping The Holy Trinity. Child, you have found favor with I. Not because of your lack of sins. Your sins were before me but now have been erased. Your faith and the greatness of your love is the fruit that blossomed in you. Your repentance is what I found acceptable so WE accepted your fruit and now I have saved you and sealed you eternally. I wept as joy filled my spirit before GOD! My sins were forgiven! Joy wrung thru out heaven as the angels rejoiced. The prodigal son has returned. The black sheep has joined the flock and a great protector is born. The angels sung these words as they echoed thru out heaven. Take my child to John thundered The Holy Trinity. I felt power lift me of my knees as I was worshipping and looking at The Holy Trinity. I was lifted up by 2 in white who glowed with long hair and beards. They looked like the wisdom and the power of the ages was upon them. They had glorious crowns and their eyes full of grace, peace and love. I am Elijah the one said and I am Moses the other. I was so extremely happy to see them. Uncles I said such love is in my heart for thee. We know they answered we have watched you since birth. There has been battles done on your behalf between heaven and hell. I didn't ask why? I knew all things will be revealed so I hug them both and thanked them. We entered the room that was again never ending with no ceiling or walls yet you felt you were in a section or room because there was privacy and couldn't see the rest of heaven or the heavenly hosts. John, Elijah thundered in voice, brother called out from Moses spirit. I am here John replied as I heard water flowing the sound of a waterfall. I looked and there was a waterfall gold and in brilliant lite thundering yet peaceful at the same time. The water rolled off the fall but peacefully and smoothly. The liquid glowed and looked like liquid gold.

There, next to this great waterfall, there was John the Baptist. As we approached the waterfall it became smaller instead of larger. That was very strange to me. As we got closer to John the waterfall became smaller and smaller. By the time I hugged and kissed John the waterfall was my size. It was like a perfect fit. I asked John to baptize me. He led me into and under this perfectly sized waterfall. It fit my body and was pouring down right above my head. You are forgiven of all that is ungodly. I John baptize you in the name of The Father and of The Son and of The Holy Spirit. You are now cleansed. John then took me by the hand out of the waterfall and I said to John, Uncle can I have a drink. For I know all things are good in heaven and there is no waste for perfection reigns with God. This gold cup like object with a long handle appears in Johns hand as he dips it into the water falling from the fall. The cup filled and was offered to me to drink. John said drink and you shall never thirst again. For now, you are cleansed thru and thru. I drank three times from the cup each time giving thanks to the Holy Trinity. Go in peace child and visit me anytime you will. I am here. Come said Moses and Elijah took me towards the direction of travel. Where are we off to uncles I replied. The Lord asked us to take you to the room of knowledge so that you may have all your questions answered and all shall be revealed to you. It will not be in a book your answer come from for there is only one great book however you will witness your answers manifest before you and all your senses will experience the answer to your question as well. It will be written within you and you shall never forget. As we hovered or walked thru heaven we suddenly were outside or what seemed to be outside. I saw the new Jerusalem as a whole in the distance celebrated like a bride going to the church. She glowed and was in heavenly glory. She seemed to be at a distance but up high for all to see her splendor. As we walked I saw my earthy father who had slept in Christ. He smiled at me and asked me telepathically how are you brother? All is perfect I answered with no voice and he smiled as he kept going to where he was going. Then I saw David speaking to Solomon both with their crowns of glory. Walking like to friends consumed with a conversation as it seemed important. Now there was no need for anyone to tell me who each being was. I knew for I recognized them from within. We all knew each other without having to introduce each other. This happened after my baptism from John. As we went thru the gates into the outer court we started walking thru the garden of Eden. Eden was alive and breathed with every breath of God in harmony. There was grass, water, trees, fruit and heavenly food. Others were there walking, sitting others were eating. There were angels and there were heavenly citizens. All together in perfect harmony. Everything in heaven is perfect and there is no waste. So even though there are no females or males or sexual organs. Even though there is no husband or wife but just children of God others looking young others old. Others like females and others like males we were all the same. Everything you ate or drank was good. There were no bathrooms or need of one. For all things that were consumed stayed within and used by your new super body. You felt no pain or sorrow. There are no tears but everyone is always rejoicing and praising God. There were others fishing and eating fish. In the distance rolled from up high a blanket unfolding or rolling down. There were meat and food it was all good and given by God for all to choose and eat. I tasted the fruit and tried the meat and it was all in heavenly delight and perfect. So much in fact that all of my senses rejoiced and were occupied at the same time. The scents were incredible. You can smell all the fruit at once in harmony or all the meat or fish. It was all good. It is nothing on earth that can compare to the splendor. There was manna and bread. There was wine and water pouring out from waterfalls for you to drink. You never were full yet always satisfied. There was nothing bad or expiration dates on anything. All was good and eternal. There was the tree of life and its fruit. All would eat and the angel wasn't there to protect it anymore. It was available for all of heavens citizens. You accepted by hand and ate yet you never got dirty nor did you need to shower. We all smelled like life! death was defeated and nowhere to be found. As we walked we entered into a room that seemed to be exclude to the far left of heaven. As we entered into it became a meadow with grass short in stature and a glow above like a son. Where are we? I asked Moses and Elijah? I felt like I was back on earth but in a place of beauty and right over to the right what seemed to be the Grand Canyon. I heard the sounds of horses and from above my head I saw four horses with their riders. Behold the four horsemen. The horses seemed to have wings but had none. They had different colors each. One was red the other pale and white. One was dark and black and the other dead and I can see its bones. It looked like a skeleton with skin. The riders were gruesome and death was upon them. I didn't fear as they road above our heads they came down to the meadow and their horses seemed to eat. Except for the horse that seemed dead. The horses breathed fire and

His brothers and sisters. So even though our Lord had no blood brothers or sisters for Mary knew no man ever, he did have brothers and sisters under titles of respect. Brother and sister were the common name for all children of Israel to relate to each other. Holy Mary mother of God is her title now and forever. Unblemished pure and eternal. We walked Jerusalem and witnessed the Lords death on the cross. The devil being at watch everywhere not knowing what was to happen next. He even tried to touch the Lords spirit as it was given up to God by Christ himself and was hit and thrown back by a great surge of power. In those days all who died or most who died were taken by the devil to the pit. When Christ died on the cross, He went down and released all souls from the pit where the devil had them. This was the first resurrection of the dead. Christ went down and preached the truth as Lord and Savior. The souls of the peoples of the past repented and worshiped him and the Lord released them into heaven as their tears of repentance poured forth out of them. All knees kneeled before Christ and God redeemed His people and took back all authority and control. All the authority lost by Adam was taken back by Christ from the devil in a swift blink of an eye. The devil was so angry. He thirsts for our blood from the very beginning. He quickly called out to his legions and generals for a new plan of action. Paul and I listened as the devil spoke to his demons on the new plan to gather man's souls and fill hell once and for all. Permanently fill hell. He brought forth all the five senses and created plans that will through all into sin. Utilizing their senses as doorways for their destruction. The demons were given authority to constantly follow and tempt everyone. They are constantly around people all the time. They use the ears to tempt and program man. Continuously whispering thoughts of sins while awake but most of all while sleeping. They were told to put ideas into man's heads with whispers. We shall tempt them with their eyes and program them with their ears the devil explained. With their hands and touch we shall stain them guilty of the blood of the innocent and use their hands to commit sins of the flesh. We shall give power to their flesh and squeeze the light of God out of their souls so we can consume their souls with our darkness when they die. We shall tempt them all thru their senses and turn them into the gate ways to hell. These will be none as the deadly five passages to hell. Man is a slave to the sins of the flesh. Marniere, teach man to use different plants to experience their power while inhaling them or smelling them. The affects will be toxic to their bodily parts. It is then when we shall possess them easier. How replied jashiros? In their weakest state they are ours for the taking and well squeeze the life out of them. The sins of the flesh will be a powerful weapon against man. I will take charge of that replied Legion. I shall stand with you replied ashereas. More gathered with legion at that time. It involves all sense explained the devil. Yes, ruler slithered vertiose. I understand. The more senses we get them to use, the greater the habits and sins become. Program man and woman to love each other instead of the opposite sex. Show them the pleasures of the flesh and use others who serve us, to do the same. Teach all the people occupying the ground how to use all things God created. For their own death. Consume them all. I want to get drunk on their blood. The devil spoke and created his plan with the fallen ones and Paul and I listened.

solid wings and blew out his breath and clouds separated and came to gather in the distance in darkness. Thunder and lightning from heaven came into them and rain poured down on man. The other angel went up and twisted and the clouds and air became a cyclone and tornado in a spinning power and touched down on the earth. The other angel grew in stature and blew wind with such power that it separated the ocean into a dry path as it was done for Moses for him and his flock to cross. The other angel cleared the clouds as he blew the wind and the sun rained down on the earth. I smiled at the angels and thanked them for their introduction. We walked with Paul and we seemed to have gone closer to the earth into this great stench. It was horrible the smell was deadly and toxic it made me feel like I was going to get sick and throw up. Paul what is that awful smell I have never smelled it before but it feels like I'm going to die if I keep inhaling it. Its making me sick. Paul replied, it is the sins of man as it gathers up into the atmosphere and creates storms and hurricanes of death. The sky wants to cleanse itself from the stench and the angels provide the wind so the smell can be destroyed. But man keeps sinning and the angels keep working with the rest of creation to rid sin from the world. Man's sins and abominations are before God and the stench of death and evil. I did see these bright lights and wonderful scents coming up from the floor of heaven to the throne of God before. Those are the prayers of repentance and of the Holy children of God. It is like incense before the throne of God. That stench is the sins of man and leads to death. Yet if you look over there, as Paul said this I turned and saw the demons rejoicing in that They seemed like they were bathing in it. They would point down to man and bet with each other one soul for another and who will be able to cause him or her to commit the worst sin. The winner would have first crack at the soul's suffering. Stench. It was like a drug to them and they were getting high. They were breathing it in and were happy. The winner above all others would be the demon that would cause them to commit suicide. That's the ultimate win. There is no greater than the one who caused the apostle to betray Christ and commit suicide and betray God. That demon is well known and holds the trophy. The greater the servant that falls, the greater the victory in hell. In a wink of an eye the demons rejoicing in the stench of man's sins saw us and came to us with fury and at the same time a dinosaur with great wings and fire flew straight up from the bottom of our feet to our faces. Paul stepped forward before all of them as I was safely behind the apostle. Why are you still here the demon screamed? Who is he and why are you protecting him Paul servant of the highest. Paul smiled at them and said, be gone with all of you. How dare you come before us. Paul spoke in an angelic or heavenly language. He then summoned fire and lightning from heaven and it rained down on all of them. They wept, screamed, hissed and begged Paul to stop. It seemed like fire full of acid burning them. Yet it was alive and it covered them all like blankets. It didn't harm Paul or myself. I actually liked it. I felt stronger and more powerful. They all retreated and flew away as quickly as they could from us as they became invisible. Also, that fire cleansed that stench that was there from the sins of man. The fire and lighting came together and took form as I came before us and said I AM! I didn't have to ask Paul I knew it was Holy Spirit. The giver and taker of life. We smiled at each other and continued our walk. As we walked I asked Paul. Why did the Jews reject Christ even though they were waiting for their Messiah? Why did they not recognize Him? Come I shall show you my thorn in my side that caused me such great agony. We suddenly were in Jerusalem and the people were rejecting Christ. Do you see? I saw demons whispering and manipulating the Jews and telling them what to do what to say. They were on their backs like monkeys talking whispering tempting, smirking wicked smiles. They were telling them He is not the Messiah but a false profit. They said he is a demon and works for us. He uses magic, don't believe him. He is just a man acting like God. He is a sinner and a friend of the tax collector and the sinners. Look how weak and pathetic he is. He can't save you they whispered to the Jews. He can't even hold a sword how is he going to liberate you. It kept going on and on. Demons everywhere like herds of cattle. Tempting, and lying. Whispering and pushing them all threw there five senses to even commit murder. Behold my thorn. I saw the days of past and Jew murdering Jew under the umbrella or word God. To find righteousness in their thirst for blood which was heavily manipulated by the demons. All it took was one thing for the formula to be completely and for murder to occur with demonic influence. Anger, jealousy, lust, depression, sorrow and judgement. When these seeds were available in man then getting man to murder became easy for the devil and his followers. They can easily have man or woman murder someone else or murder themselves. Suicide is self-murder influenced by pure evil. Paul showed me the demonic manipulation of the ages even Stephens death the first martyr. Forgive them Father for they know not what they do. Then I confessed to Paul my sins. I was married twice and failed in both marriages. I watched pornography and committed sex acts before marriage and after my divorce. I have lied to people and have cheated them. I have been jealous and envious. I have over eaten and turned my back on people asking for help. I have suffered with anger and masturbation. I was ashamed as I told these things to the Apostle and tears of repentance covered me for all my sins, like I was under a waterfall. I am a sinner I proclaimed yet the Lord chose to save me. Paul replied, it is the nature of your repentance and the great love you possess for The Holy Trinity that is the foundation of your rebirth. Now that you are born again. Great power will come upon you from The Holy Spirit. All things will now change and you shall know and understand God. Now you will think more like God and a lot less like a man. I thanked Paul as He reminded me that we all have thorns and crosses to bear. The difference is those who come to the cross in repentance and those who do not. We are not God just men. We are all things in Christ and nothing but dust without our Savior. It is the fact and the truth. What about the generations of Isaac and Ishmael? I asked Paul. They are already under Gods wrath. They can't and won't see God unless they belong to the Son. After they go thru the cleansing process and remember that all things are possible with God they will enter into different sections of heaven. Even though they will hear God they will not see Him or be near Him in heaven. They will be in the outer court of the kingdom. The inner court, is for Gods children. All those who have accepted The Son. They will sit at the table and feast with all of Gods children eternally. The feast will be one of spiritual gifts from the Father that shall fill their souls and new bodies for all eternity. Then the rest as Paul spoke he told me to leave out the rest that which he revealed until another book. I listened and lowered my head remembering feeling sorry for those who will miss out on Gods full glory. Paul lifted my chin and said there is always hope. God sends His helpers. You are one of them. It is your job as it was mine to tell them that are dead the truth. Show the blind the truth. Teach the learned the truth. Raise the dead, heal the sick, bring forth the name and power of The Holy Trinity to the shameless world. Those you forgive will be forgiven in heaven those you judge guilty will not be forgiven. Be careful how you exercise this gift. Nations shall heal and retentive tears shall pour forth for judgement day is already hear. Even now all is almost ready for the Second coming of our Lord Jesus. This time he comes as The Power of God and the Judge of all creation. Our time has passed and we walked and before I recognized what has happened The Apostle John was with me. Come child John said I will show you that which is written in the final chapter of the scripture which is the fulfillment of the creations that must die so that they can be fulfilled and glorified in fullness and take their place eternally in heavenly glory. All things must die in Christ so that they may live eternally in Gods glory. As we walked John showed me the churches and the evil abominations occurring there. The killing of Gods servants as their blood spills behind the walls of the alters. Satan ruling the false religions as they all worship the devil unknowingly. He manipulates the elect and programs them to like and molest children and even have sex with the same image. Male with male. Female with female. Even females looking like males or males like females with surgical procedures that cause one to be neither male or female. All these sins and abominations. God created all in perfection. The devil wants to destroy that perfection with the forcing of sin and teaching sinful knowledge. All with his whispers and programming. Man is quick to judge and to murder just like the devil is. If you don't serve God, whether you know it or not, you are serving the devil. It's one or the other. There is no in between. You are either a child of light or a demon of darkness. That is the whole reason for the second plain. It is the souls cleansing process to enter into heaven and come before God. If the cleansing process wasn't available, all will turn to dust before The Holy Trinity because of their sins which are deep scars on the souls Look at Moses. Great servant of God. Yet upon the mountain God said you shall not see me from the front but you may seem me from behind. Moses would never had been able to withstand Gods purity and would have turned to dust. Even as Moses witnessed God from behind he still aged instantly. Holy Spirit is pure love and innocence. If one would blaspheme Holy Spirit, there is no forgiveness. Wo unto him or her that call evil good and good evil. The devil and the demons are guilty of blaspheming the Holy Spirit. There is no forgiveness for them even if they repented. There are two deaths. The death of sin which is our flesh and the death of soul which is our spirit or ghost. The flesh is already judged and must die because it is sin. Unless you are like some prophets or saints that overcome their flesh and its sin. They walk the earth in the spirit close to God. We all walk in the world in the flesh as we are all sin and must die so that we can live. Sin is not anywhere in heaven. Forbidden, not allowed. It doesn't exist ever since satan and his followers were thrown out. You must be cleansed. You are stripped from the sin or the flesh. The soul goes under purification and healing in purgatory and then on the day of judgement you receive your new body and your name will be written on your forehead by the hand of God. At that given time where no one knows only God, there will be a new heaven a new Jerusalem a new earth and the garden of Eden will be open to all citizens. All will be made new. Including man! When free will exists, it can guide you into different directions. Others good others bad. Who decides what's good or what's bad? Look into your heart. A murderer can consider murder as good as satan does. I healer would consider healing and saving life good and not bad. You see, according to whom you serve and what is written in your heart is your determination of good and evil. Only God is good because He is pure love and perfected life-giving power. Satan kills, lies, destroys, but in his eyes, he is the power. All those sins and things he offers are not good. He blankets himself with greed, jealousy, pride, betrayal of anything that is pure and innocent and much worse he does to his loyal followers. Giving the right circumstances, we can all be trained or programed to be good or bad. To be straight or gay. To be wicked or loving. It's just a matter of how many senses are used as we are being programed. People commit sexual sins and watch pornography. It is like smoking a cigarette or cigar for the very first time. The body goes into shock. After your chasing an excitement. You drive yourself into new things maybe child pornography or having sex with the same sex. Sit and watch pornography while under a heighten emotional or aroused state and before long you will act out in reality that which you witnessed others doing. If its sex with the same sex, you will fantasize about it, the devil will whisper to you at night while your sleeping and he will bring the right person of the same sex across your path. He will even arrange for the right mood. Remember the demons watch and take notes all the time. They know your weaknesses and your strengths. They expose and feed on your weaknesses and chop down your strengths until there is nothing left and you are consumed in shame and sorrow. Sin has come out of the closet and it is committed openly now. Good is now called abnormal and evil normal. It is easy for a pure soul to be a victim to the flesh of original sin passed down thru the bloodlines. The worse the bloodline the harder for the next born to overcome. Man has the ability to take perfection and change it to imperfection. That occurs in the mothers' womb with the first beat of life. Why does God even continue to give the souls? To purify the blood line. That's where the Saints come in. They purified the blood lines by overcoming their flesh which is sin and has accumulated the scars of their fathers' sins.

That is why their bodies, even upon their sleep, do not turn to dust. They will wear their bodies as trophies forever in the new heaven. Their bodies have been cleansed by their own hand and Gods help of course. Let me explain the truth in simplest form. God and His word and The Holy Spirit existed and was is and shall always be. God created all things with His words. God's word is alive. All things were created with His word and command. Now, God saw man's sins and knowing man can't exist in his sinful form before the purity and love of God, without disintegrating, sent His word to become flesh who is His Christ. The only Son of God, Jesus. Who is God because He is Gods words in flesh. Believe in my Son sayth The Lord our God who paid for your sins in full. Believe in Him, have faith in Him, hope in Him and let His blood and flesh heal you and save you. Do so, repent in truth and live sayth The Lord our God. My Son is the only true path to Me sayth God. Do you know understand that the only way to live and be close to God is thru your faith, belief, hope in His Word who is Jesus The Christ and true repentance? Repentance is saying to God I'm sorry Father that I hurt you with my sins please forgive me and help me with your mercy to overcome them for your loves sake. Baptize them in the name of The Father and of The Son Jesus and of The Holy Spirit is Gods command. Why? It is a show of faith on our part and belief in The Holy Trinity. This is our gesture of repentance and showing God our love for Him. Receiving Holy communion is our cure and forgiveness. Confession is what releases your spirit from the weight and burden of your actions that violate Gods purity and love for you. Which is the only thing that is real and full of life in this world and in heaven. Then once the good fight is fought and the path traveled, God welcomes you into heaven as a son and not as a creation. Why? Because His words flesh and blood that is eternal who is Christ, lives within you eternally and can never die. The Lords flesh, the Lords blood is within you and has covered you. In this manner the Lord The word of God has cleansed you and sanctified you. Now since God is eternal and Christ that lives in you is eternal has made you eternal. That is why we are called the body of Christ. We are His physical body blood and flesh and can't die. We have consumed our Lord physically and spiritually make us His. His actual body.

Believe in our salvation who is Christ and live. You walk in heaven and have been forgiven. If you don't accept Gods sacrificed word who is Christ for your sins, but because you kept Gods commandments that are written in all of us in our hearts, you might get into heaven, because all things are possible with God. However, you will not know or see God. You might hear Him or sense Him, but you will never sit at the table with God. You will be in the outer courts of heaven. There is only one way to The Father and that is thru Christ Jesus our Lord, our Savior, our God. Period! This is not negotiable. So yes, you might walk in Eden or on the new earth or even the far ends of heaven but you will not be near God. You will not be part of the immediate family. Nor will you receive the blessings of the eternal Lord. You see, hell has different levels one stacked upon another like an ice-cream cone and has an end. Heaven has different levels but all spread out infinitely like a big blanket without a beginning or end. Imagine how far you can actually be from God, hanging out with others like you. Not reaping the full benefits like Gods children who are the body of Christ. Free will has caused imperfection. Thru Christ, your free will that leads to accepting Him in Truth and as the Truth full of Grace becomes your salvation and perfection. This gives you full access to all of creation. Reject Christ and you are under Gods wrath. Maybe if you get into eternity you will be limited because your free will has guided you to incompleteness. You have not accepted God in His fullness. You only accepted part of Him. You have rejected His Word and His Holy Spirit. Your faith becomes incomplete and you only have wrath to endure because of your sins. Remember, you can't survive physically or spiritually in front of God.

You will turn to dust. Remember what happened with Moses. He was a great servant and is a great servant but he couldn't withstand seeing God even from behind let alone being judged by God and facing Him. We are nothing like Moses so imagine what will happen to us without Jesus Christ. We have no chance. I'm telling you the truth please hear me. After what seemed to be a while and Paul who is fully known, knows fully, answers and secrets hidden thru out the ages were finally revealed. The things I was told can fill more than seven books. I am guided per. I followed Paul and we went to the cities of the past. Sodom has no glory and the descendants of Caine ruled there. The city was covered in darkness even during the day. I saw the demons possessing and manipulating men women and children. However, I noticed that man actually liked it and did not resist. I saw fire fall from the heavens as all were turned to ash caught while in there filthiest of sins. Like a child's hand in the cookie jar. The angels bared witness to the sins who stench was so bad that it reached heaven. I saw the angel of death as he passed over the houses marked in blood as he took the first-born lives from the inside out. Then we came across this powerful water. I saw Moses as he came to the water with Gods flock and as a good shepherd he asked all to have faith. All were either scared or angry thinking that they shall die. They heard the cries and screams of their captives as they approached them. I saw the devil riding with the Egyptian king and demons everywhere around them. Moses lifted his staff after he prayed and from the corner of the planet came a huge angel that seemed as if he had huge wings that can cover the planet itself if the angel chose to do so. The angel seemed to be about 30 feet tall.

He looked at Moses and the flock. He looked at the approaching Egyptians and demons that had the devil himself as leader. The angel then lifted his head to heaven and said Father bring glory to your name! the angel looked like he took a deep breath and flapped or clasped together his wings and blew out wind with such great force not seen by man or felt by man ever. The force of wind was so powerful that it tore into the ocean separating it into two halves. Moses took his flock thru the opening. Now here is the thing. As the water split as the wind from the angel cut thru the water and separated it, the wind itself also split and blanketed the water as a wall to stay fixed as they all passed. Once they were all to safety the angel pulled the wind back into himself and the waters were once again whole. They didn't come together slowly. One moment the waters were separated the next the water was a blanket covering its territory once again. Those Egyptians that drowned were sealed in their graves. Paul then took me by the hand and we walked on the water. Behold the ark and a new beginning. I witnessed and marveled at the size of the ark. There were 2 of creation there for God had opened the windows of heaven and poured water on to the earth that wiped out the evil and the evil doings of satan and the fallen ones. The giants were done with, so were the watchers and all those whose heart was wicked and unjust. All righteous and innocent were on the ark. The ark was a rebirth and a new beginning. However thru out the years the blood lines were mixed and on the ark the bloodline of Abraham was alive and well. Noah is a just man and serves God with love and obedience, even now. More so than his family and their wives. The blood lines were mixed for his sons' wives had

Ishmaels bloodline mixed as well. God fulfilled his promise because even with a new beginning God had told Abraham that His descendants will be more than the stars and more than the sand on the shore. I looked at Paul as we walked on the water and around the Arc. We entered and witnessed all that had remined of creation in the whole world was inside the arc. Nervous yet trusting and waiting upon the Lord were all. Even the animals were nervous yet at peace at the same time not causing problems but instead lying with each other awaiting word from Noah. I told Paul I would be nervous as well because I knew not what to expect being on the arc and waiting for land. However, I would find peace that God doesn't break promises. I trust in the Lord. So even if I'm nervous at times, my faith and love in The Holy Trinity overcomes all worries and fears. There you have it! We are all descendants of Abraham. The promise that God made to Abraham was for all of us who came after the flood. So are the blessings. Anyway, God gave them all long-life lines to repopulate the world. As their families grew and the world began to repopulate there was an expansion into the land which was one large peace at the time. Paul and I continued on the journey and we came across the land where the tower of Babel was being created. Man celebrated and at that time they believed God was not there or showed no interest to the level the people of the time demanded. Let us build a tower to heaven where we would not need God in this life or to let us in on the next life. God new their hearts and heard their words and allowed them to build a very high tower going into the sky. Now, they would have never reached heaven anyway however their intentions were wrong. They even criticized the power of God and soon they were not afraid or respectable any longer towards there heavenly Father. So that God can teach them a lesson He waited upon the tower being free and clear of workers and took His hand and swatted down on the tower from heaven as one would hit a mosquito on their hand. The Lord crushed the tower into dust and His hand struck the earth causing it to break from one piece into many big peace's. They all wondered and spoke to each other yet no one, no longer understood each other for God had given them all the knowledge of language to each a gift of a language. Immediate understanding was between family bloodlines. Every man woman and child spread out against the lands as they drifted into the waters and the lands carried them to different sections of the plant. It was interesting to see that they were specific distances away from each other and very difficult to get from one to the other without a boat. Remember that the oceans were occupied by the creations of the deep. As time went on and man populated the world and as they all spread out, God commanded the ocean floor to open up and for the volcanoes to rise so that they created land as man needed it in time. As I witnessed all things created Paul and I were marveled with the perfection of God. Just like heaven is never ending and continuously growing and expanding, so is the universe and so is all of creation. Paul said that the day of judgement is a day where all creation will be judged and all that is old will be made new in eternal perfection accordingly to Gods' will. Even though originally all was created perfect and good, because of sin, free will, or manipulation from the devil and his follower, that which was good was cursed by God and it must die for violating Gods word. That is why on the day of judgement all will be made new. All that will live of course. Everything else will be discarded. Behold the sun that is alive and feeds off its own energy and eternal flame, will one day be nothing but a flickering candle light that will be blown out. Since God created all things with His word and that word became flesh and is His Son Jesus the Christ, then it's obvious that the Lord created all things with his touch. Doing so with love and grace. All things created by God the Father, God the Son Jesus and God the Holy Spirit even though separate yet still one rested as they blessed their creation and said it was good. All completed in 6 days. Imagine the power of the creator. We also are like the creator because our words create as well. We also create our destiny according to our free will and actions taken. Paul blessed me as we had returned back to the point of heaven when we first started our journey and smiled. As Paul disappeared from view another glowing like a son with power in his eyes and a face of an innocent child and man appeared before me. Timothy, he said come with me I have much to show you. Who are you I asked mesmerized by his glory. I am he who wrote revelations for this is Gods warning and call for the elect. I am John. I greeted the apostle John and hugged him. He embraced me with a Holy Hug and wrapped his arms around me as angelic wins and said. It is time to reveal to you that which is to come and that which is to do. I walked with John and the floor of heaven opened and we walked right into the second plain that is under heaven. I can hear the angels signing and glorifying God yet all my senses besides my hearing were now not in use. Before I was in continuous ecstasy because all my senses were in full use and now I felt cold, alone and desiring to be with God. My heart felt sad and yet eager to go to God my Father. It is the same for all here Timothy. When you are here you can hear the angels and Go and you desire to be in heaven. The punishment for your sins is the period you wait as you desire to be with God and the rest of your heavenly family. Is this purgatory? I asked. Yes, replied John. Here is the rest and cleansing stop for the souls that will get into heaven that have not truly repented as of yet. It broke my heart as we saw all weeping and praying and waiting for judgement day so that they can get in. As we walked we heard prayers for all by the saints in heaven and prayers coming from what seemed to be the floor of the second plain. Behold said John, the prayers of the saints comfort them like a blanket and the prayers from the churches and loved ones on earth cloth them. As we walked I saw all those in purgatory awaiting and then I saw a whole other section in the second plain completely cut off from the first. There I could not here anything else but the voice of an angel. I witnessed the angel reading the old and new testament scriptures to a mass of souls. It's interesting because it was of one heavenly language and all were on their knees listening and weeping. The angel kept teaching and the souls kept listening and weeping. What is going on here I asked Paul? These are the descendants of Abraham said Paul. They are here to listen to the truth until judgement day. Will they be saved? I asked Paul eagerly. Paul answered and told me not to write down what he said in this book but the next which will be on salvation. I agreed and Paul told me what is to become of the Jewish souls and the Muslim souls that were sitting all together as family members listening, weeping and hearing the truth again and again as they did on earth and never accepted it. Now they know the truth and weep. That is there punishment. What about their spiritual leaders for the Jews or the prophet of the Muslims and their leaders. They are all guilty of killing the innocent in the most inhuman manners. So, with every word the angel reads of the old and new testament, it is etched into their souls as if written on skin. Are they suffering or in pain? No actually the eternal words of God are soothing their own suffering. I don't understand I replied eagerly to John. You see my child, they rejected the truth even though the Lord our God sent them teachers to help them. They killed and martyred Christians all over the world under there false beliefs that there's is the only truth. There is only one way to God and it is thru His Son the only Christ who is God. This is Jesus. They rejected Him even killed Him. So, did the Muslims who share the same wrath of God as the Jew. Both the seed of Abraham. It is Abraham himself who agrees to an even stricter punishment that awaits them. I saw them in hell as well. Those in hell are demons or are being transformed into them. Those that you see here are those who are good at heart or have been tricked by the devil. Those that did not do any physical harm to others yet watched others do it instead and rejoiced. They are still guilty of sin. For, even though they might not have spilled innocent blood themselves, they are still guilty of it because they did nothing to stop it either. Will they ever be saved or get into heaven? Do not write this down in this book of seven. It will be in another. John gave me the answer to my question and we walked passed them all. As the angel kept teaching them the truth they kept listening and weeping and asking for forgiveness. We entered another section and we found another angel teaching the old and new testament to a whole other group of souls. John answered before I asked and smiled. Timothy, you are so eager to know all things and I see the great love you Have for The Holy Trinity and your heavenly family burning uncontrollably within you. We all love you as well. I dropped my head as John said this. I don't know why maybe I was shy or lovingly embarrassed. These are the followers of buddha and the other false religions in the world today. All good people with peaceful beliefs blinded to the truth. Gods words as the angel speaks is being written in their hearts. They are weeping and anxious as they accept the truth. They however have a longer process for their healing. After the truth is written in their hearts, they are then guilty of sin. Then they will move into the second section where we found the Jew and the Muslim and then into the first sector where they will await judgment. Oh, I see, even in purgatory the further you are from heaven's door the more you suffer and long to be with God. So those in three must go to two and then gather and wait in sector one. I got it. Thank you I replied to Paul. Still remember all things are possible with God. The saints and heavenly hosts are praying for all of them. What about their wives or their children or family members. They are all here with them. However, there is no family relations or any other type of relations in the second and first plain. We are all children. Is your family here I asked John? I have never known a woman nor have I ever had children. I have remained pure and serving God. I unlike others were given the gift of not desiring to have any type of relations physically or mentally. Was that one reason the Lord said you were His favorite and most loving disciple? The Lord does favor purity and virginity. With focus on

God alone. You see I explained to John. That is why sometimes I am angered with man. There is a whole section of Christianity including Muslims atheist, Jews and so many more that speak against The Virgin Mary and believe lies. That she was a regular woman that she didn't remain a virgin that she had more kids etc. That makes me so angry. If sinful man can go in life without experiencing any form of sexual desires or actions, how much more can a Holy Vessel of God? That is where the devil's manipulation has a strong hold and keeps them who might get into heaven away from sitting at the same table with God. According to your beliefs you will be spaced away from the Holy family explained John. I am not angry with man for they do not know nor understand but I am furious with the devil and all his followers. They have done a lot of bad since their creation. However, the outcome of some of their bad actually turned to be good for the faithful for they received blessings from God for overcoming the hours of testing. Yes, said Paul we the created all serve the creator in one way or another. Whether we willfully do it or not the outcome is always beneficial for that which is good. We must think like God and not as man. No matter how creative and evil the devil becomes and his followers, no matter what evil they thrust upon the world there will always be an equal or opposite reaction to the action. For every action there is a reaction. When the devil possesses ungodly people, who have the thirst of death within them he causes them to terrorist acts of destruction. However, all who serve satan will end up dead anyway for he shall kill their flesh. Their souls are jeopardized and usually end up in death as well. So, fear the creator who can kill body and soul and not him who can only destroy flesh. We had terrorist attacks throughout the planet from evil servants of the devil programmed to kill and destroy. Towers have fallen thousands are being killed. There is so much pain and suffering brought on to us from the devil and his followers. Why not wipe them out as God wiped out man with the great flood? That was different. The flood did not wipe out all the bloodlines. The day of judgement will come and all evil will exist no longer. Until then there is hope prayer and repentance. If you are a father and you have two sons. One is good and one is evil, which shall you condemn to death or hell? I understand. The day of judgement is the final hour. It is left up to the created and there free will to choose until the given time of judgement. Yes, but until then people suffer. Man is to occupied with that which does not matter and not occupied with that which matters. Man's faith is less than a mustard seed. There words full of lies and false promises consumed in greed and sexual acts. Not everyone is immoral but I have seen man's abominations and your sins are before me sayeth the Lord. Yet still I love and I wait. But the time is running short and I come as a thief in the night. Prepare yourselves for the day of judgement is at hand. John asked, who is in greater judgement he who knows or he who knows not? Obviously, I replied, he who knows more. Then why are not those who serve God even in the churches that are committing all forms of sins not trembling with fear. I guess because they have Christ I replied. It is written that the Lord shall throw into the darkness where there is gnashing of teeth these so-called servants and they shall be no more. You are afraid to exercise your authority but the gifts of Gods spirits are all over you and within. What are you waiting for? Why are you rebellious asked Michael who suddenly appeared by my side when I was speaking with John? I am not trying to be rebellious but I am a sinful man and I am afraid I answered to Michael. We were all afraid at one time or another replied John. Even Michael faced fear before great power came upon him from Gods spirit to overpower the devil and throw him out of heaven. Fear, is nothing but lack of faith and not knowing the outcome of something that you feel is impossible or such a great task. What is impossible for God? Nothing I replied. Then what is there to fear? Nothing I nodded my head in agreement. I guess we just all need to surrender. Surrender what asked John? Our free will and allow the Holy Spirit to fill us with Gods will. John and Michael smiled. Bring him to Me thundered the voice of God throughout heaven. Johns eyes had what seemed to be lightning sparks coming out of them as his body seemed as polished brass and he glowed as the sun decorated in heavenly glory. Michael is tall in stature and very powerful with a face that glowed. He looked like a young man full of confidence and authority. By the time God finished the word Me, we were before His throne and God himself. God now looked like an older man with longer hair white in color and gold blended with in as he glowed in such beautiful perfection. There is life, creation, love, kindness, peace, power, righteousness, grace, mercy, forgiveness, vengeance, fire, punishment, judgement and death in his total beauty and perfection. He is fine polished brass with the energy of life and light glowing and pushing out from within Him. All of creation can be seen circulating within him as a robe in the shape of a body. He is beautiful and perfect. I have never seen such beauty and perfection as The Father and the

Son have. We in fact are in their image but not in their glory. I feel we wouldn't be able to handle their power. Man is self-destructive in one way or another. The smell of all creation and the prayers of the faithful was occupying all the space around the throne and the Holy Trinity that I was in ecstasy as I took breath in. The lord came to me and said. I shall give you crowns of glory as my elect. Choose your first. As God waved His hand I saw crowns in His hand and I said. I am not worthy of any of them Lord. If I am to wear a crown it shall be no greater than yours. Now God knows what I have in my heart. As I was speaking The Lord smiled and before I was done a crown of thorns was in his hands. God the Father looked over and said You will be known by three names. One for the Greek, one for the Catholic and one for the Jew. Then the Lord placed the crown of thrones upon my head. It didn't hurt at all but instead it made my full being glow. Even the tears running down my face were like gold liquid drops. Your heart is one with mine. I saw the Lord take what seemed to be a spiritual heart with a crown of thorns and He put it in me. Literally his hand with the heart went right into my body as if I had no physical form at all. Then the Lord blessed me and laid His mighty hand upon me and said. The time is coming it is already here. Gather on to me my flock and go to the churches. There hour of judgement is at hand. You will come before them and say blessed is he who comes in the name of the Lord. Stay with them if you must for three days. I shall take care of the rest for I shall judge them swiftly and my judgement shall tear into them like a two-edged sword tears swiftly anything it comes across and goes into. My fire is in thee and my spirit upon thee. If they deny thee they deny

I Am Alpha and Omega! The Beginning and The End,
The First and The Last!

Me. I Am! I come with great power and glory. My judgement is my sword and the time where all shall kneel before the truth is here. You are not to bring peace to the earth or the churches as my servant of the past have done so. You are to bring a sword. You are my warrior and my judgement is in thy hand in righteousness. I bowed my had and accepted my assignment as God showed me more things. What I am to do, where I am to go. He showed me the near future and the future not so near. I accepted all that there is to come and The Holy Trinity blessed me. The Holy Spirit came upon me and blanketed me like a dove with great wings and sealed me within. As I rose up after The Holy hug, I was witnessing a great war in heaven before my very eyes. It seemed as one would sit and watch a movie. Angel against angel. Lucifer and Michael at arms wrestling with each other. Michael had great power and so did the other angels with Michael. Gods voice thundered in heaven be gone before me lucifer and all who are yours. You have broken my heart. Let the earth be your resting place and the spiritual realm where you wonder. You are not welcomed in MY house No more! As Gods voice thundered in heaven, what seemed to be the floor of heaven opened and before any angel knew what was happening while they battled with spiritual swords and shields, heavens floor opened and lucifer like lightning was thrown out of heaven and so were the other rebellious angels. They actually seemed like spiritual lightning as they transformed into darkness. There light was torn out of them. Then the floor closed and they were all gone. All the spiritual wounds on the remaining angels all healed instantly before God and heaven was back to an immediate peace. As if nothing ever happened. Then

Michael and Gabriel, Raphael, Uriel approached this group of angels who did not involve themselves with the war in heaven. Michael went up to the leader and said. You have all lived out to your name doing justice to it. I shall keep watch over all you watchers. I sense you are up to no good. Before long, you shall not be welcomed here either. Uriel agreed and Gabriel came up to them and said we sense your betrayal already and Raphael spoke and said that the time is coming that you shall be no longer occupants in Holiness but servants of the damned. Gabriel replied and said there is time for your repentance. Go speak to our Father. You are all already becoming darker and the light of life is diminishing from within you. The watchers earned their name that time when they witnessed the battle of lucifer and his followers trying to take Gods throne by force and picked no side. It was the perfect time for them they thought because The Holy Trinity was in the third plain creating the world and then man. Man, who is Gods greatest creation. Lucifer was foolish thinking God can't see or know all things. So, he and his followers rushed the throne room but found Michael, Rafael, Gabriel, Uriel and the other warriors on guard. Dressed for battle and prepared. All was peaceful in heaven and I went for a walk of all that is made new. As I walked The Apostle Peter was by my side. I turned and saw him in heavenly glory and smiled. Come with me he said and I turned and followed him into the room of that which is to come. God has chosen you not because of your lack of sins but because of the greatness of your love. Heaven rejoices over the greatness of your love. Your repentance along with your love has filled heaven with the sweetest scent. This is why you have been chosen. Behold what is to come and judgement. I saw and witnessed the future and judgement day. As Peter spoke he told me not to write down that which is revealed to me yet but instead in the other books and to separate the knowledge given to me as The Holy Spirit guides. I saw the two pillars of God with great glory preparing the flock and protecting it from the antichrist. I saw the underground and the hiding places of those who did not receive the mark of the beast. Then Peter showed me that which is to come in my life. The scroll was opened in his hand and I witnessed my life and my death and my life once again. I hesitated and wept and then I accepted that which was shown before me. When I did so, the fear of death haunted me no more and all was clear as the scroll was rolled back up and I ate it. It became one with me. It was written in an angelic language that is alive and gave me strength so that I can finish the good race set out before me like a red carpet. Ever since that day I am able to speak a language not known to man but only in heaven and for the first time ever, I am truly able to express myself completely with thought and word. We kept walking with Peter and we walked on the water and allowed ourselves to sink down up to the waist. I asked again about the dinosaurs and the length of time or age of the world. Peter drew out a gold net and placed it into the water. He said grab on to the net and let us fish together from this day forth. I held unto the net that glowed of gold made with gold strands and we were talking to each other about things of the past things to come. Peter replied that the dinosaurs were the devil creating in his image. He is that ugly and angry, disgusting and violent. So, what he is on the inside was what the dinosaurs looked like. It's an automatic reaction to an action that he has not been given right to. What about scientists who are taught how to calculate time that tell us the earth is millions of years old as oppose to thousands of years? I asked Peter? Even though the formulas the devil taught them are still incorrect their method of time calculation is both wrong and right. How so I asked eagerly? There calculation is wrong because whatever the number is that man gets its much greater than man thinks or has the knowledge to calculate. It's not the age of those things created by God that are millions of years being calculated but the DNA of God. I don't understand. God created all things and all things came from within God and His word. Yes, I replied. The measures of age that is being calculated of the things that God created and the things that came from God and are Gods' is a false reading of the age of The Holy Trinity's existence. I understand know I replied. Peter smiled. I asked Peter, where is the Lord? Look there! Peter replied. Father is on the boat. The Lord and the rest of the Apostles are there I pointed and asked eagerly seeking? I saw the Lord and the Apostles from afar as the Lord glowed like a sun. Yes! Come I said to Peter let us go. As I prepared myself to swim to the boat with a forceful underwater dive under the bright stared sky, Peter stopped me and said wait! It is not your time yet! There is still much for you to do. The water was like liquid crystal that was calm and up to my chest in depth. The sky was dark and the stars bright. You can clearly see the whole universe above us in heavenly glory. Peter smiled at me and blessed me as He touched my forehead. I was instantly before the Holy Trinity. I was on my knees and asked God must I really leave? God then picked me up as a child. I sat on His lap and the Lord blessed me and said. Be not afraid for even

I Am Alpha and Omega! The Beginning and The End,
The First and The Last!

though your task is great I AM always with thee. The Lord kissed my forehead as one would a new born baby. That moment I woke up and remembered everything ever since. I have not come to bring peace on earth, but a sword! I remember thinking. What a dream? so clear and alive. Then again, was it a dream? To be continued in a series of seven! Until the next! God bless you and all whom you love!

Printed in the United States
By Bookmasters